Acclaim for Robert DeVinck
Author of *The Pono Principle*

*"The author's voice is welcomingly frank, and his
thinking deftly draws on a surprisingly wide array of
sources . . . Readers of New Age philosophizing will find
the blending of traditions here appealingly done. . . .
A touchingly personal and heartfelt account of transforming a
me-centered view into something more peaceful and fulfilling."*

- Kirkus Reviews

*"The Pono Principle distills man's never ending search for peace
and happiness into one simple sentence. Do the next right
thing, always. It brought me great comfort, and guidance."*

- Robert Dugoni, *New York Times* best-selling
author of *The Extraordinary Life of Sam Hell*

Also by Robert DeVinck

THE PONO PRINCIPLE (2017)

THE ASCENSION WITHIN

BECOMING WHO WE ALREADY ARE

Peace & Aloha,

Robert DeVinck

ROBERT DEVINCK

BALBOA.PRESS

A DIVISION OF HAY HOUSE

Balboa Press books may be ordered through booksellers or by contacting:

Balboa Press
A Division of Hay House
1663 Liberty Drive
Bloomington, IN 47403
www.balboapress.com
844-682-1282

Print information available on the last page.

ISBN: 978-1-9822-5025-6 (sc)
ISBN: 978-1-9822-5026-3 (hc)
ISBN: 978-1-9822-5024-9 (e)

Library of Congress Control Number: 2020918258

Balboa Press rev. date: 09/23/2020

To Bill W., Dr. Bob, and the Fellowship, for catching
me when I fell into the abyss - but, more importantly,
for holding my hand as I took the necessary
Steps towards Recovery and Resurrection.

*The descent into the depths always seems
to precede the ascent.*

- C. G. Jung

*All spiritual growth is no more than a matter of
becoming who we already are.*

- Fr. Richard Rohr, OFM

CONTENTS

CONTENTS

PREFACE

For half a century, I was on a personal quest to rediscover the important things that I knew as a child but had lost (forgotten) along the road of life while "growing up." My journey was a tedious one, primarily because I had limited my search to the world around me, trying to find Truth, God, Happiness, Love and Peace, somewhere "out there." It was a big world, and so it took me many decades of transplanting myself all over planet Earth, while also beseeching the heavens above, for answers to life's most important questions.

Yet, somewhere within me - specifically in that foggy cavern of my mind where memories are filed away - I would sometimes have a momentary recollection of a childhood thought, or feeling, that would answer these questions I was searching for. What did I know then, that I didn't know now anymore? I needed to find what Ken Wilber refers to as my "Original Face" - the Face I had before my parents were born. I started to feel like Peter Pan in Kensington Gardens who, after only seven days of being a human, had trouble remembering what it was like being a bird, which is what he was truly born to be. Like Peter, I felt like I was a "Betwixt-and-Between," trying my best to remember that, as a child, I too knew how to fly (at least, in my dreams).

Thus, my personal journey was never meant to be an external one. The answers I was looking for were never to be found in distant lands, or in books, or in other people - and certainly not within the egocentric False Self that I had created over a lifetime. After all, how can "Truth" ever be known by a "False" Self? One day, my journey brought me to the edge of a towering precipice. The long road on which I had journeyed had come to an end - and none of life's important questions had been answered for me.

In desperation, I jumped. And in that suicidal act of killing my False Self, I resurrected my True Self, the essence of who I truly am.

What Baal Shem Tov so wisely said became my newfound truth: "Let me fall if I must fall. The one I will become will catch me." Only then did I rediscover the answers that I knew as a child – but only by searching within my own "innerness." As I opened the treasure chest that was buried deep within me, I reconnected to an indwelling God, who had been there all along, ever since my creation. I rediscovered an inner Peace and Happiness that I had long ago forgotten I possessed. I once again found what true Love is, and am now able to clearly recognize Truth when I see and hear it.

I was 57 years old when I killed the selfish, self-centered alcoholic that I was. My resurrection occurred the day I walked into a recovery meeting and began the internal journey to rediscover my True Self, the person that God created me to be. I have enjoyed a sober mind, a healthy body, and an awakened spirit, for ten years now, and what I have learned from my inner journey is contained in the following pages.

My fervent prayer is that the life lessons I have learned may be of value to you, the reader, as you continue on your own personal journey, confident that after every fall, no matter how challenging, you have the ability to ascend again. How, you ask? That's easy. By basically becoming who you already are.

Robert DeVinck
Maui, Hawaii

INTRODUCTION
(Coming Home)

Her name was Gloria, and she was born in the early spring, on an Easter morning. Her mother was nursing her when her father arrived at the hospital with Gloria's 4-year-old sister. After kissing Gloria on the top of her head, the father held up their older daughter so that she could get a good look at her new baby sister. As Gloria continued to nurse, her older sister smiled and said, "Mommy, she looks like a little angel. Can we take her home?" Those were the first words ever spoken to Gloria by her older sister.

The home in which Gloria lived during her early childhood was in a beautiful rural area, many miles outside the large metropolitan city in which her father worked. When he was offered a substantial promotion within his company, the family moved into the city, where Gloria and her sister were enrolled in a private school. By the time she became a teenager, Gloria had trouble remembering their first home in the country – the pond where she learned how to swim, and the tree house that her father built in a large maple tree which overlooked the pond.

Unlike her older sister, who was a high school honor student, Gloria was very rebellious and had a difficult time with authority. When she told her parents that she refused to wear a school uniform any longer, they had no choice but to transfer Gloria to a public school near their home in the city. Her strong will didn't serve her any better in the new school, where she was always being disciplined for skipping classes and not turning in assignments.

By the time Gloria started high school, she was hanging out with a group of older kids who had introduced her to alcohol and drugs. What started off as weekend parties of beer drinking and pot smoking, quickly morphed into other drug experimentation and stronger alcohol use. Gloria had an older boyfriend, who lived in a shabby apartment with two other boys, and she often fought with her parents after she didn't come home at night. It didn't take very long for her substance abuse to destroy her relationship with her parents and older sister. Her addictions had completely taken control over her, and her family felt helpless in the face of it.

At the age of sixteen, Gloria dropped out of high school, said goodbye to her parents, and left home. Her older sister was away at college, so Gloria didn't see any point in telling her about her decision. Her parents were completely bereft and shattered. As they stood at the front door, watching their younger daughter drive off with her boyfriend, on the back of his motorcycle, Gloria's mother sobbed uncontrollably as her husband held her. Gloria was leaving home, and they had no idea where she was going – and neither did she.

Over the next two years, Gloria was completely cut off from her family, along with everyone from her past. No one knew that she had travelled to the other side of the country, broken up with her boyfriend, and lived on the streets of a large urban city. She often panhandled for money, immediately using it to buy cheap booze and drugs. The inner-city streets were a dangerous environment, and Gloria knew that she had to learn how to survive, or she would surely die.

During those same two years, Gloria's parents sought counseling to deal with their grief. They also attended a recovery group for families of alcoholics and drug abusers. With their older daughter finishing her last year away at college, and not having any idea as to the whereabouts of Gloria, their 25-year marriage was strained beyond measure. What solace they found in praying together could not assuage their greatest fear – that, for all they knew, Gloria could very well be dead. It was that frightening possibility that haunted them every day. They felt empty inside, as they tried to endure their common suffering within the emptiness of their home.

On Easter Sunday, Gloria's parents went to church. Even though this particular Easter fell on a different date than the one when Gloria was born, the moveable feast of Easter was, for them, a validation of their strong faith in God, and their special connection to Gloria. Before leaving the church, Gloria's parents lit a candle, knelt before a statue of the Blessed Virgin Mary holding her baby Jesus, and prayed that their lost daughter would someday return to them.

Over the next two months, Gloria's older sister was preparing to graduate from college. She was proud of the fact that she was able to maintain a 4.0 GPA throughout her entire four years of study, even while working several jobs during those years. She couldn't wait to receive her diploma, and to see the pride on her parent's faces as she received special recognition for graduating Summa Cum Laude. Her graduation from college was, without question, the biggest achievement of her life, and she was so glad that it was only a few weeks away.

When her parents arrived on Graduation Day, the campus was abuzz with activity as everyone was beginning to assemble at the football field, where the commencement ceremony was to take place. The students were lined up, on the field, in long rows of white chairs, while family members sat on the bleachers in the stands. Before taking their seats, her parents went to look for a vendor to buy bottles of water. As they stood in line, the father noticed a young woman in the distance, walking towards them, holding an infant in her arms. She looked familiar to him and, without saying anything to his wife, he began to slowly walk towards the young woman. As he weaved through the large crowd, trying not to lose sight of the woman, their eyes suddenly met – it was Gloria!

In a burst of unbridled emotion, Gloria's father ran through the mass of bodies that separated him from his lost daughter, wrapped his arms around her, and held her tightly. With tears in her eyes, Gloria looked up at him and said, "Dad, I'm so terribly sorry to have hurt you and Mom the way I did. Can you ever forgive me?"

"Oh Gloria," he repeated several times, as he kissed the top of her head, "We had no way of knowing if you were even alive. I can't begin to tell you what joy I have in my heart right now. God has returned you to us." As he spoke these words, his puzzled gaze fell upon the small infant that Gloria was holding between them.

"Dad, this is Grace," she said, turning the baby's face towards her father. "She's the greatest gift God has ever given to me." Seeing how dumbfounded her father was, she added, "She was born two months ago, on Easter Sunday, just like me. I'm not with her father anymore; he's completely out of our lives now. I'm in an addiction recovery program and have been completely clean and sober for almost a year now. I was hoping that I might be able to come home again, just long enough to get back on my feet."

"Of course you're coming home with us," said the familiar voice of Gloria's mother, as she ran up and threw her arms around her daughter, weeping with gratitude. "Our prayers have been answered. You are alive and well and have come back to us." She looked at the infant in her daughter's arms, and said, "And just look at this precious little angel you have here."

Gloria carefully handed the baby to her mother and said, "This is Grace, Mom. She is the gift, and promise, of my sobriety. She is the reason I am alive today."

With that, the reunited family went to watch the commencement ceremony. When Gloria's sister first saw her, after the ceremony, she was initially reluctant to embrace her. Her memories of Gloria, during her early teenage years, had filled her with huge resentments - and these resentments had eaten away at her over the past several years. But when Gloria offered to let her hold Grace in her arms, her heart opened up and her resentments slowly melted away.

Only after hitting rock bottom was Gloria able to face her addictions, take the requisite action steps to confront them, and consequently, keep them at bay one day at a time. With the loving care and support she received from her family and recovery group, she was able to rise above the wreckage of her past into the light of a promising, and promised, future. With a clear and sober mind, Gloria found herself seeing life through the innocent eyes of her beautiful daughter. For the first time in years, she was able to remember the country home she lived in as a little girl - of swimming in the pond with her sister, and playing in the tree house, which in autumn, was set amidst a spectacular canopy of radiant maple leaves.

In the span of only a few years, addiction had all but killed a beautiful child named Gloria. She was completely lost to herself, and to her family. In finding the tools to combat her addiction, she eventually found her True Self, and was able to come home again. God's gift of Grace saved her.

CHAPTER 1

GOD (HIGHER POWER)

Therefore there is only one problem on which all my existence, my peace and my happiness depend: to discover myself in discovering God. If I find Him I will find myself and if I find my true self I will find Him.

- Thomas Merton

We are stardust - physically born on an infinitesimal planet, floating in an infinite universe - thus sharing the DNA of the universe. We come into this world in our purest form; every newborn child shares this purity of essence. In the same way that one particular child, born beneath a star in Bethlehem, brought into this world Peace, Joy, Love and Light, so too does every child born possess these same gifts within themselves. Yet, despite being "equipped" with these internal life essentials, we are born totally defenseless and dependent upon this new world we have been delivered into. From the moment we take our first breath, we must rely on the love of others in order to survive. Without other loving beings to feed, care, and nurture us, we would die.

We are also born with thinking minds. This is what separates us from rocks, oceans, and trees. Our earliest thoughts are our most innocent, and precious, ones. As a spotless vessel of pure love, we trust that we will be loved in kind - simply because love and trust are all we know. Like sponges, we absorb all that we see, hear, and sense around us, and then process that information through our infant (yet ever growing) brains. When we are hungry, too hot, or uncomfortable, we cry as a sign that we are not feeling loved. When a loving caretaker satisfies our needs, we become happy and content again. Love is all we want, and love is all we need.

I believe that deep within the physical body and mind of every newborn child is an eternal soul, our link to our Creator God. Because I believe that every person is made in the image of God (*imago Dei*), it follows that we also share His DNA as well. Before the birth of Jesus Christ, God was looked upon as a Divine (although distant) Being in the eyes of the faithful. He was always somewhere "out there" - up in Heaven, high on a mountaintop, or speaking down from the clouds. Franciscan sister and scientist Ilia Delio states, "God is not a super-natural Being hovering above earth, but the supra-personal whole, the Omega, who exists in all and through all."[1]

Naturally, the last place anyone would ever think of looking for God would be *within* his or her own soul. That changed after the Incarnation of Jesus.

The Promise of Divine Indwelling

Just before his arrest in Jerusalem, God's Son in human flesh tried to comfort his disciples by assuring them that He would not leave them "as orphans" after His death. He did this by explaining to them the covenant of Divine Indwelling. He first makes sure that they understand that He and his Father are one: "Believe me when I say that I am *in* the Father and the Father is *in* me"[2] (John 14:11, NIV). He then promises that they will come to know the Holy Spirit, whom God will send in Jesus' name, for the Spirit "lives with you and will be *in* you"[3] (John 14:17). Lastly Jesus says that, after His death, "you will realize that I am *in* my Father, and you are *in* me, and I am *in* you"[4] (John 14:20) [emphasis mine].

Jesus is basically confirming to every living person that the Divine Presence of the Holy Trinity (Father, Son, and Holy Spirit) is not to be found "out there" somewhere, but right here *inside*

2

each and every one of us. Nowhere is Jesus more specific on this subject than in Luke 17:20-21 (KJV). When Jesus was asked by the Pharisees, when the kingdom of God would come, He answered them: "The kingdom of God cometh not with observation: Neither shall they say, Lo here! or, lo there! for, behold, the kingdom of God is *within* you"[5] [emphasis added]. Far be it for me to ever attempt to "read" more into the words of Jesus than was intended, but in this one particular verse, it appears to me that Jesus is clearly saying, "Quit looking out *there* for the kingdom of God - for it is right here *within you.*

I suspect that, as we grow out of childhood, we forget what we so clearly *knew* at birth (but didn't have the ability to communicate) – Heaven is inside of us!

A Dutch Painter Helps a Dutch Priest Find the Home of God

In one of his most insightful, personal, and powerful books, *The Return of the Prodigal Son* (1992), Fr. Henri J. M. Nouwen discusses his spiritual journey following his first viewing of Rembrandt's painting of the same name. Like most people, Nouwen sought God somewhere *out there*: "I tried constantly to point beyond the mortal quality of our existence to a presence larger, deeper, wider, and more beautiful than we can image."[6] In other words, he tried to get a glimpse of God in all the "familiar" places - in the "loneliness and love, sorrow and joy, resentment and gratitude, war and peace" - all the varieties of human experience to be found in the world. But the Dutch-born Catholic priest soon discovered that he was on a spiritual pathway that was leading him in a different direction, to a different place:

> *I have been led to an inner place where I had not been before. It is the place within me where God has chosen*

3

to dwell. It is the place where I am held safe in the
embrace of an all-loving Father who calls me by name
and says, 'You are my beloved son, on you my favor
rests.' It is the place where I can taste the joy and the
peace that are not of this world.

This place had always been there. I had always been
aware of it as the source of grace. But I had not been
able to enter it and truly live there. Jesus says, 'Anyone
who loves me will keep my word and my Father will
love him, and we shall come to him and make our
home in him.' These words have always impressed me
deeply. I am God's home!

But it had always been very hard to experience the
truth of these words. Yes, God dwells in my innermost
being, but how could I accept Jesus' call: 'Make your
home in me as I make mine in you'? The invitation is
clear and unambiguous. To make my home where God
had made his, this is the great spiritual challenge. It
seemed an impossible task.

With my thoughts, feelings, emotions, and passions, I
was constantly away from the place where God had
chosen to make home. Coming home and staying
there where God dwells, listening to the voice of truth
and love, that was, indeed, the journey I most feared
because I knew that God was a jealous lover who
wanted every part of me all the time. When would I be
ready to accept that kind of love?

God himself showed me the way. The emotional
and physical crises that interrupted my busy life at
Daybreak compelled me - with violent force - to return
home and to look for God where God can be found - in
my own inner sanctuary. I am unable to say that I
have arrived; I never will in this life, because the way
to God reaches far beyond the boundary of death.

*While it is a long and very demanding journey, it is
also one full of wonderful surprises, often offering us a
taste of the ultimate goal.
When I first saw Rembrandt's painting, I was not as
familiar with the home of God within
me as I am now.*[7]

Many Paths To The Summit

Having been born less than two months after the first ascent of Mount Everest (by New Zealand beekeeper Edmund Hillary and his Nepali Sherpa Tenzing Norgay), I have always had a deep fascination for that particular historic event. While in New Zealand, in 2017, I had the opportunity to go to several museums and learn more about the 1953 British Everest expedition that ultimately led to the summit of Everest. One of the things I learned was that there were originally only two routes up Everest, the South Col and the North Col. Today, there are 16 additional routes that have been taken, for a total of 18. This fact got me thinking about the interfaith teachings of Sri Swami Satchidananda, who would always say that all of the world religions were seeking Truth/God, but just following different pathways in their search: "Ultimately, we all aim for the same truth while walking on different paths."[8]

After visiting the Sir Edmund Hillary Stairwell Collection of artifacts at the Otago Museum, in Dunedin, I returned to my hotel and began to explore the connections between the many different paths to the summit of Mount Everest, and the many paths to seeking Truth/God. What I discovered was amazing. As there were only two major paths to the summit of Everest in 1953 (i.e. the North and South Cols), there are also only two major world religions that have a membership of over a billion followers (Christianity and Islam). But it was the next bit of research that absolutely floored me. As I studied the list of other world religions,

I discovered that there were 16 additional religions that had a membership of over a million followers, for a total of 18. One summit, many paths. One God, many paths.

For the record, the 18 world religions (each comprised of over a million adherents) are as follows:

1. Christianity (2.1 billion)
2. Islam (1.3 billion)
3. Hinduism (900 million)
4. Chinese traditional religion (394 million)
5. Buddhism (376 million)
6. Primal-indigenous (300 million)
7. African traditional and Diasporic (100 million)
8. Sikhism (23 million)
9. Juche (19 million)
10. Spiritism (15 million)
11. Judaism (14 million)
12. Bahai (7 million)
13. Jainism (4.2 million)
14. Shinto (4 million)
15. Cao Dai (4 million)
16. Zoroastrianism (2.6 million)
17. Tenrikyo (2 million)
18. Neo-Paganism (1 million)

To my complete surprise, I had discovered that, over many years, a small number of humans had succeeded in climbing 18 different routes (or paths) to summit the world's highest mountain, while the vast majority of humans also sought 18 different ways to find their highest power or ultimate truth. In the same way that it interests me what particular path a mountaineer takes to summit Mount Everest, it, likewise, is of interest to me to know what path someone takes to achieve spiritual enlightenment or Divine Consciousness. As important as the ultimate accomplishment is (i.e. ascending

Everest or finding God), I find it much more fascinating to know how a Christian, Buddhist, and Hindu can each come to the same understanding that we are all here on earth with only one mission - to love and serve one another.

This is why interfaith symposiums are so valuable to our communities - and why religious tolerance is so very vital to our human experience. It is only when we expand our knowledge of other world faiths that we are able to grow in our own. A dear friend of mine once told me that he is a much better practicing Catholic because of his study of Buddhism. I have found that to be true for me, as well. No better example of a transformative East meets West spiritual moment exists than what happened at the summit of Mount Everest on May 29, 1953.

The Cross At The Top Of The World

Earlier that year, Father Martin Haigh, a Benedictine monk at Ampleforth Abbey, North Yorkshire, sent a small crucifix - given to his father by Pope Pius XII - to the leader of the British Everest expedition, Colonel John Hunt, before the historic 29,028-foot climb. He wrote to Hunt, asking, "I would be deeply grateful if you would leave this little crucifix at the highest point your expedition reaches, if possible at the summit itself."[9] Colonel Hunt replied to Fr. Haigh: "I was very moved by your letter with its little enclosure. I feel, like you, that this venture has a deeper inspiration than most of us openly admit to and that we shall succeed only if we keep that basic motive uppermost in our minds."[10] Hunt told Fr. Haigh that it would be a privilege to carry the crucifix as high up Everest as possible, asking only for the priest's prayers "from mid-May onwards."[11]

On May 27th, on the South Col at 25,800 feet, Colonel Hunt handed the small envelope containing the crucifix to Edmund Hillary, saying, "And so, Ed, the main thing is to get down safely, but

I know you'll get to the top if you possibly can!"[12] At that, Hillary put the envelope in the pocket of his windproof, where it remained for the next two days as he and his Sherpa colleague Norgay continued their arduous climb towards the summit of the world.

At 11:30am, on the morning of May 29th, two men stood at the top of the world for the first time. One man was a fair-skinned New Zealander, the other a dark-skinned Nepali. One man was a Christian, the other a Buddhist. But the two men were tied together with one rope, and for that reason they always, humbly, maintained that they had both reached the summit simultaneously. Physically, they took an identical pathway to the highest point on earth. After shaking hands and hugging each other in mutual congratulations, Hillary began to take photographs from the summit of Mount Everest.

"Meanwhile," Hillary observed, "Tenzing had also been busy. On the summit he'd scratched out a little hole in the snow, and in this he placed some small offerings of food - some biscuits, a piece of chocolate, and a few sweets - a small gift to the Gods of Chomolungma which all devout Buddhists (as Tenzing is) believe to inhabit the summit of this mountain. Besides the food, I placed the little cross that John Hunt had given me on the South Col. Strange companions, no doubt, but symbolical at least of the spiritual strength and peace that all peoples have gained from the mountains."[13]

And so it was, that although these two men represented two different religious beliefs, they shared in an identical demonstration of thanksgiving to their individual God. Shortly after the expedition, Fr. Haigh received a letter from John Hunt, letting him know that his crucifix was "placed upon the highest point" of the world. The importance of that simple act of thanksgiving was not lost on the Benedictine monk, when he replied to Colonel Hunt: "I am sure that when that history comes to be read, the day when men climbed to the summit of the earth and left there the sign and symbol of our faith, will rank as one of the very great days in the history of the world."[14]

Ascending To Our God Self

The Ascension is actually the birth of the Inner You
expressed as the spiritual individualism of the inner
particle state.

- Stuart Wilde

I am in a constant state of ascension - not only because of all that has happened in my life - but also in spite of all that has happened in my life. By definition, most would assume that the pathway of ascension is upward. I have found the opposite to be true. Whatever glimpses of enlightenment I have had, whatever spiritual growth I have experienced in life, have only been realized by my journeying inward, deeply *within* myself. In *The Soul's Journey Into God*, written in 1259 AD, Saint Bonaventure holds that knowledge of God is innate in the soul of humankind. He uses the term *soul* to refer to "the image of God in the depths of the person, the most profound dimension of man's spiritual being."[15] St. Bonaventure purposefully did not use the Latin phrase *ad Deum* (to God), but the much bolder *in Deum* (into God), to emphasize that God is already *within* us, awaiting the spiritual pilgrim to ascend *into* Him.

The other common *assumption* made on the subject of *ascension* (see what I did there?) is that one does not spiritually ascend to his/her *God Self* until one has physically died. Who says? My personal experience has taught me that my state of ascension is taking place now, in this moment in time. What happens after my death is anyone's guess (with heavy emphasis on the word *guess*). I certainly don't pretend to know what happens to my body, mind, or soul after my heart stops beating and I stop breathing. What I do know is this: every day that I consciously choose to move further away from my *False Self* (*Ego Self*), I become closer to God - and to the man God created me to be (i.e. my *True Self*).

My personal ascension towards the realm where God resides within me began when I started to follow His gentle whisper.

9

Since time immemorial, humankind has longingly searched the heavens for God - or Gods, as the case may be - for isn't that where one would naturally look? God "spoke" to man in booming thunderclaps, "beckoned" him from the majestic clouds atop tall mountains, and "rewarded" him by making it rain on his parched farm fields. Throughout history, man just figured that God must be *up there*, somewhere, right? Yet, in the Holy Bible, when Elijah is told to stand on the mountain because the Lord was going to be passing by, we are told: "Then a great and powerful wind tore the mountains apart and shattered the rocks before the Lord, but the Lord was not in the wind. After the wind there was an earthquake, but the Lord was not in the earthquake. After the earthquake came a fire, but the Lord was not in the fire. And after the fire came a gentle whisper"[16] (1 Kings 19:11-12, NIV).

It wasn't very long ago when I realized that, to hear a whisper, especially a gentle one, an individual must be very close to the person speaking in order to hear what he/she is saying. That's when I remembered the old adage that the ego is the distance we put between God and ourselves. During these past ten years of addiction recovery, I have been sincerely trying to bridge that gap between me and God, by destroying my False/Ego Self - that facade of a man that I used to be. Over time, I began to notice how attuned my ears were becoming to God's gentle whisper, and that's when it hit me: for me to be able to hear such a soft, quiescent voice, it must be coming from *within me* and not from the heavens above.

If one believes that humankind was created in the image of God *(imago Dei)*, or that God *breathed* life into man, then one can readily understand why many world religions, and mystic traditions, believe that each of us is born with the *divine spark* of God within us. I believe that it is that divine spark that whispers to us from that place within our God Selves. In the same way that our Ego Selves loved to tell us how wonderful we looked on the *outside* - how smart we were, how rich we were - all of those superficial (i.e. *exterior*) "qualities" we prided ourselves as having, it was only when we began

10

to mine deeply within ourselves that we found our true God-like, Divine Essence.

As a spiritual pilgrim, on a personal quest to ascend to that place where God dwells, I have come to realize that I could spend a lifetime traveling to the far reaches of the earth - from Tibetan monasteries in the Himalayas to St. Peter's Basilica in Rome - only to realize that, at no time, was I ever traveling alone. For wherever I was on my "solitary" journey, looking for God in the resplendent majesty of nature, other people, and temples of worship, it was only when I looked within my True Self that I began to ascend to where God truly lives - within the temple of my soul, ever whispering, gently and lovingly, "Welcome Home."

The Perennial Tradition and Divine Indwelling

The Perennial Tradition, a term coined by German philosopher Gottfried Leibniz, and developed by mystical universalist Aldous Huxley, is "the psychology that finds in the soul something similar to, or even identical with, divine Reality."[17] It represents a universal spiritual truth, shared by a multitude of world religions – Christian mysticism, Islam, Zen Buddhism, Hinduism, and Taoism – that humans desire to connect with, and experience, the divine. In his book, *Immortal Diamond* (2013), Fr. Richard Rohr explains The Perennial Tradition thusly:

> *The Perennial Tradition, the mystical tradition that I*
> *will be building on here, says that there is a capacity,*
> *a similarity, and a desire for divine reality inside all*
> *humans. And what we seek is what we are, which is*
> *exactly why Jesus says that we will find it (see Matthew*
> *7:7-8). The Perennial Tradition invariably concludes*
> *that you initially cannot see what you are looking for*
> *because what you are looking for is doing the looking.*

> God is never an object to be found or possessed as we
> find other objects, but the One who shares your own
> deepest subjectivity - or your 'self.' We normally called it
> our soul. Religion called it 'the Divine Indwelling.'
> Some will think I am arrogantly talking about being
> 'personally divine' and eagerly dismiss this way of
> talking about resurrection as heresy, arrogance, or
> pantheism. The Gospel is much more subtle than
> that. Jesus' life and his risen body say instead that the
> discovery of our own divine DNA is the only, full, and
> final meaning of being human. The True Self is neither
> God nor human. The True Self is both at the same
> time, and both are a total gift.[18]

On the subject of Divine Indwelling, University of Toronto professor Dr. Jordon B. Peterson writes, in *12 Rules for Life* (2018), "You have a spark of the divine in you, which belongs not to you, but to God. We are, after all - according to Genesis - made in His image. We have the semi-divine capacity for consciousness. Our consciousness participates in the speaking forth of Being. We are low-resolution ('kenotic') versions of God. We can make order from chaos - and vice versa - in our way, with our words. So, we may not exactly be God, but we're not exactly nothing, either."[19]

Returning to Fr. Rohr, in one of his Daily Meditations, entitled *Divine DNA* (2017), he continues to expound on the idea of "God as Us:"

> Christians worship Jesus because he did not forget but
> fully lived the union of human and divine. We, too,
> are both human and divine - at the same time. We
> dare to believe that God has become one of us, fully
> one with us - and in Jesus reveals God's self even
> as us! . . .

*I am not saying that I am the exact same as God, but
I am saying God's Spirit objectively resides in me and
in you! The divine DNA is in everyone and everything
God has created 'from the beginning.' . . .
If we continue to focus on our unworthiness and
original sin as our foundation, we will continue to act
accordingly. If Christians emphasize retribution and
judgment, we will only contribute to more violence
and division. We become what we believe ourselves to
be. Yes, I know I am weak and objectively unworthy
of God's mercy. But I simultaneously know that I am
totally worthy - and my worthiness has nothing to do
with me! When looking at me, the Creator sees God's
beloved child. God cannot not see Christ in me . . . as
the unique incarnation called 'me.'[20]*

Joni Mitchell was right when she said, "We are stardust." We
were created by God from the dust of the earth, the same dust that
fell from the stars, and the same cosmic dust that comprises the
entirety of creation. We were not only created by God, but, most
importantly, in the image of God. Our genetic makeup connects
us to all of creation - and also to our Creator. So, whenever you
find yourself questioning your self-worth, remember that you carry
God's Divine DNA within you. Whenever you feel lonely, or in
need of someone to talk to, remember that God is a mere whisper
away. And, whenever you are down, when life is beating you into
the ground, remember that the blood of He who was beaten, and
then crucified, flows through your veins and pumps through your
heart. It is He who will lift you up, and together you will ascend to
the Father who awaits within your innerness - and with open arms
will embrace and welcome you home.

CHAPTER 2

TRUTH (REALITY)

Truth lies within ourselves: it takes no rise from
outward things, whatever you may believe. There is an
inmost center in us all, where truth abides in fullness
and to Know rather consists in opening out a way
whence the imprisoned splendor may escape than in
effecting entry for light supposed to be without.
- Robert Browning

What (or Who) Is Truth?

Then Pilate said to him, 'So you are a king?' Jesus
answered, 'You say that I am a king. For this purpose
I was born and for this purpose I have come into the
world – to bear witness to the truth. Everyone who is of
the truth listens to my voice.' Pilate said to him, 'What is
truth?' After he had said this, he went back outside . . . .
- John 18:37-38

I n *A Philosophical Dictionary*, Voltaire states, "It is a pity for mankind that Pilate went out, without hearing the reply: we should then have known what truth is."[21] I beg to differ with Monsieur Voltaire in that, just because Pilate didn't wait for an answer to the question doesn't mean that Jesus hadn't already given the answer, less than a day earlier, at the Last Supper, to the apostle Thomas: "Jesus said to him, 'I am the way, and the truth, and the life'"[22] (John 14:6).

Perhaps the reason that Jesus didn't answer Pilate was because of the form of the question posed to Him; had Pilate used a different interrogative pronoun and asked, "Who is truth?," maybe Jesus would have given him the same answer he gave to Thomas the night before. To paraphrase Ayn Rand, Jesus could have responded, "Who is truth? This is truth speaking."

The Christian belief that Jesus is "the truth" is a profound one, suggestive that all truth is to be found in Him alone. As a self-defined theistic rationalist (but one who also believes in the Divinity of Christ), I accept as truth the words that Jesus spoke to Thomas. But there is also a part of me who sees truth much like Hemingway's mortally wounded character, Robert Jordan, at the end of *For Whom the Bell Tolls*, who observed: "There's no one thing that's true. It's all true."

What (or Who) is Truth? I am on the road of life to find out, ever listening to His voice along the way, as He guides me toward the truth.

*   *   *

What you have just read is something I wrote in July 2011, on my blog entitled *My Road To Truth*. Back then, I wrote under the pseudonym "homoviator" (i.e. man on a journey). Like many other spiritual pilgrims, I wasted many years looking for truth somewhere "out there" in the world. The supreme irony is that, whatever spiritual *insight* I discovered "out there" - while traveling the globe studying world religions, mystical practices, and spirituality books - ultimately led me to the inner sanctum where all truth resides - within my True Self. In other words: THE TRUTH IS NOT OUT THERE.

To be clear: I'm not suggesting for a moment that there aren't a multitude of constant solicitations, everywhere you go, directing people to join "the one true religion," or to vote for the "only truthful politician" on the ballot. We seem to go through life believing that truth is to be found in university libraries, or in a particular poet's verses. We quote the Holy Bible and the Quran when we want to reference truth, and some are even willing to die in support of the words they are referencing.

Unfortunately, many of today's "truth seekers" are unconscious of the fact that many of their sources are merely propaganda mills, pumping out biased views that have absolutely nothing to do with truth. Of course, the art of propaganda is in the dissemination of false information that connects with the visceral fears and emotions of a populace. During the final year of World War II, on the island of Saipan, Japanese propaganda declared that the attacking American forces would "rape and devour" Japanese women and children and mutilate the bodies of Japanese soldiers. Believing this information to be the truth, over a thousand Japanese civilians and soldiers committed suicide by jumping to their deaths from Suicide Cliff and Banzai Cliff. Sadly, the Japanese propaganda could not have been further from the truth, and those poor innocents died as a result of that contrived falsehood.

The major problem with seeking truth "out there" is that you have to rely on what other people *believe* to be the truth. For five centuries, every encyclopedia and history book in the world stated, as fact, that Christopher Columbus first set foot in the New World on the island of San Salvador in 1492. But in 1986, the National Geographic Society announced that - after an exhaustive five-year investigation conducted by noted historians, archeologists, navigators, cartographers and other experts - Samana Cay, a narrow, nine-mile-long island, located 65 miles southeast of San Salvador, was the most probable landing site. Oh well, it's not exactly like Columbus knew where he was in the first place - he believed he had landed on the outlying islands of Asia, or the Indies, as they were known then.

In 2008, my wife and I traveled to the Holy Land and visited the town of Bethlehem. Naturally, the most famous site - what is believed to be the birthplace of Jesus Christ over 2,000 years ago - is the Church of the Nativity. The main entrance to the church is through the small Door of Humility which is only four feet tall and two feet wide. The Grotto of the Nativity, the place where Jesus is said to have been born, is an underground space which forms the crypt of the Church of the Nativity. After descending a flight of steps to enter the cave, one finds on the floor a 14-pointed silver star with an inscription around it which reads: "Here Jesus Christ was born of the Virgin Mary." Every day, pilgrims visiting this site will get down on all fours and kiss the spot where Jesus was born.

Naturally, a rational person might question whether this silver star *truly* marks the exact location of Jesus' birth. I'm sure that, for many, the uncertainty of that one question could possibly cause them to question the validity of the entire Jesus "story" as told in the Holy Bible. For me, personally, the silver star is merely a symbol of the birth of Jesus in the town of Bethlehem. Whether he was born in that exact spot, or 200 meters to the northwest, is completely unimportant to me. What **is** important to me are the words that Jesus spoke to Thomas at the Last Supper, "I am the way, and the truth, and the life."

And that Truth resides - not in some grotto beneath a church in Bethlehem - but in the very depths of my inner being.

In The Beginning

It was when I was 16 years old that I first heard the most profound statement about the existence of God that had ever reached my ears. In the 1969 film, *Easy Rider*, Peter Fonda's character, Wyatt, reads an inscription on the wall of a New Orleans whorehouse: *"If God did not exist, it would be necessary to invent him."* It wasn't until many years later that I discovered the origin of that statement. The French writer and philosopher, Voltaire, wrote those words (*"Si Dieu n'existoit pas, il faudroit l'inventer"*) in 1770, nearly 200 years before I heard Peter recite them in the movie.

To this rational thinker, that one statement trumps all others, and leaves every theist-atheist argument where it belongs: in the annals of wasted talk and debate. The genius in Voltaire's logic is that he took the question of God's existence out of the eternal metaphysical argument (one that has never been, nor ever will be, settled) and brought it into the light of reason. Voltaire believed that a rewarding and avenging God, a God who blessed the good in man and punished the evil, was necessary for the common good. In other words, a healthy society needed God (like children need loving and disciplinary parents), whether God existed or not. Moreover, he believed that, although man has not the reason to understand Divinity, he must see that the workings of this universe did not come from nothing and, therefore, must have been arranged by "a most mighty, a most intelligent workman." In Voltaire's *A Philosophical Dictionary*, he summarizes, "All then that I can do, without the aid of superior light, is to believe that the God of this world is also eternal, and existing by Himself. God and matter exist by the nature of things."[23]

Reason leads me to believe in an all-powerful God because, as Creator, He provides the most reasonable answer to the genesis of the universe and man (i.e. something coming from nothing). The laws of nature cry out for a Supreme Architect to rationally explain that which man has no capacity to explain. Personally, I need God in my life to thank for the many blessings He has bestowed upon me, to thank for His guidance when there was no one else to guide me, and to pray to in times of temptation, grief and suffering. I need God in my life to keep me humble.

The truth is that God's existence cannot be proved, or disproved, through reason. I am a theist because reason has led me to believe in God, not through proof (which is impossible), but through faith (which feels right to me, personally). I agree with Voltaire that, even if it was possible to know that God didn't exist, I'd still be a better man for believing that He did. In my quest for reason and truth in this world, like Voltaire, I believe that God is truth itself.

God And Liberty

There are few things in this world to which I have a personal aversion, tattoos being one of them. Of course, if certain individuals want to use their own skin as a personal canvas to draw upon, that's their business. I just don't think that my body was meant to be used as a billboard. In the same way that I find it overly self-indulgent when people feel a need to proclaim their views, on every subject, by completely covering their beater car with bumper stickers, I likewise wonder what kind of ego is at work when a person needs to share his or her worldview by having it inked onto their skin. I mean, I love my mother, but I don't need to have **MOM** tattooed on my arm so that other people can be "personally notified" that I love this special woman in my life. However, there might be one exception to my self-imposed rule. If ever I were to awaken from a stupor in a Mexican border town, to find tattoos on my body, I think that I could live with that, but only if the tattoos were two specific words. Which brings me back to Voltaire.

The crowning jewel of my personal library is my 42-volume *The Works of Voltaire (1901)*. In *Volume I*, there is Victor Hugo's eloquent oration delivered at Paris on May 30, 1878, the 100th anniversary of Voltaire's death, in which Hugo captured the essence of Voltaire:

> *Between two servants of Humanity, who appeared*
> *eighteen hundred years apart, there*
> *is a mysterious relation.*
> *. . . Let us say it with a sentiment of profound respect;*
> *JESUS WEPT; VOLTAIRE SMILED. Of that divine*
> *tear and of that human smile is composed the sweetness*
> *of the present civilization.*[24]

But it is earlier in *Volume I*, in John Morley's brief biographical outline of the life of Voltaire, where can be found my favorite Voltaire anecdote. It concerns a narrow window of time, in February of

1778, which marked Voltaire's first return to France after a 25-year exile. In the midst of the 83-year-old's triumphant return to Paris, where he was the toast of the town, Voltaire had the opportunity to meet Dr. Benjamin Franklin (on February 16), with whom he chose to converse in English. As the American commissioner to France, Franklin was no stranger to the aristocracy of Paris. But, this being his first audience before the Enlightenment's premier intellect, Dr. Franklin wished to present his 17-year-old grandson, William, and ask for the venerable philosopher's benediction. Lifting his hands above the young man's head, Voltaire solemnly proclaimed (in English), "My child, God and Liberty, remember those two words."[25]

So, in a moment when the most brilliant mind of his day sought to distill a lifetime's collective wisdom into two words, two truths, what does he utter? "God and Liberty." Those two words, gifted to a young American boy, as a blessing from an old French intellectual, said it all. The profundity, and import, of those two words go to the core of man's two greatest needs and, hopefully, to man's two greatest loves. In truth, those two words sum up a perfect existence, a perfect life. They also sum up the dream of America that had so eloquently been inked on parchment, less than two years prior, in *The Declaration of Independence.*

The dream of America was not proprietary only to Americans. After the aforementioned benediction, Voltaire shared with Franklin that he so admired America that, "if I were forty years old, I would immediately go and settle in your happy country."[26] With less than four months to live, Voltaire's last gift to an American Founding Father, and his grandson, was a sincere affirmation, and a validation, that America encompassed the truths that were God and Liberty.

At 11:15 p.m., Saturday, May 30, 1778, aged 83 years, 6 months, and 9 days, Voltaire died peacefully in Paris. Two days later, he was buried in a near-by abbey. On July 10, 1791, thirteen years after his death, Voltaire's body was moved to the church of Sainte-Geneviève, thenceforth known as the Panthéon. His sarcophagus was borne as far as the Bastille, where it reposed for the night on an altar adorned with laurels and roses. The magnificent cortège through the streets of Paris was a testament to Voltaire's eminence – a hundred thousand people were in the procession.

One of my fondest memories is when I visited the Panthéon, many years ago, with my young daughter, Geneviève (named after the patron saint of Paris). I remember showing her the beautiful frescoes depicting the apotheosis of Ste. Geneviève, before going down into the crypt to see the tombs of Voltaire, Rousseau, Hugo and Zola. Perhaps the memory is precious to me because the visit was both a tribute to my daughter, and to a man with whom I share a kindred spirit, Voltaire.

The sarcophagus of Voltaire has inscriptions on three of its sides, all very laudatory, and all written by other men. I can't help but wonder, if Voltaire could have written his own epitaph, would he have simply inscribed "God and Liberty" to represent the only two truths he was certain of in his 83 years of searching for truth? Perhaps. Would I be inclined to have those two words put on my tombstone? Absolutely. Hell, if I ever find myself back in Mexico again, I might even be willing to have those two words tattooed on my body.

True Colors

On May 25, 2020, the world witnessed the tragic death of a handcuffed black man, George Floyd, at the hands of a white Minneapolis police officer, as he knelt on Floyd's neck for 8 minutes and 46 seconds, causing him to die from asphyxiation. This gruesome, senseless murder was video-recorded for the world to see, causing an immediate tsunami of national protests and riots across America. No human being, regardless of race, can possibly watch this video without feeling totally disgusted and angry. Naturally, because Mr. Floyd was black, and the police officer was white, this particular incident possessed all the earmarks of a potential racially-motivated killing. From New York City to Los Angeles, and from Seattle to Atlanta, there was a steady stream of peaceful protests during daylight hours, only to be followed in the evening with complete lawlessness - looting, arson, and destruction of property.

For many, these riots were reminiscent of what our country experienced after the Rodney King beating at the hands of the LAPD in 1992. When the four police officers cited in that incident were acquitted, what followed in the Los Angeles area was six days of widespread looting, arson, assault, and murder. By the time the smoke from the rioting cleared, 63 people had been killed, 2,383 people had been injured, and over $1 billion of property was destroyed. "White America" had an extremely difficult time trying to understand how one incident of alleged police brutality could cause such "disproportionate" chaos. The quick answer is that this particular incident was videotaped, and the visceral effect of watching King being beaten resonated with "Black America" - because many of them have had experiences similar to King's - only theirs weren't "recorded."

I do not wish to try to explain the causes of racism, or its painful effect on people of color throughout the world, other than to say that fear is certainly one of the core ingredients. If humankind shares one common fear, it's the fear of those who are different than us - different color, language, nationality, and/or religion. We tend to gravitate, and find comfort, in what is most familiar. But what is also common is the fact that all of these differences are *external* perceptions. An individual's color, language, nationality, and religion tells us nothing at all about who that person is *inside*.

Oftentimes, when blacks and whites get together to discuss race relations, the conversation comes to an immediate impasse the moment someone says, "Well, you have no way of knowing what it's like being a black person in America." That type of a statement accomplishes absolutely nothing, other than to invalidate everything the other person was planning on contributing to the conversation. About the only appropriate response would be something along the line of, "Yes, that is correct. I have no way of knowing what it's like being a black person in America. I also don't know what it's like to be a Jewish Holocaust survivor, and neither do you. But, I *do* know what it's like to be abused, taken for granted, hated, and fearful." The "breakthrough" in that type of response is that you have shifted the direction of the conversation, by choosing not to go down the rabbit hole of trying to relate to someone *externally*, but by finding common ground, *internally*, between one another. That's the beginning of a fruitful conversation. You are no longer limited to a discussion about racial *differences* - you are now discussing where you can connect on a human level, where we are all the same color, within the *common* humanity of our inner Beings.

I remember the first time a black individual used the dismissive "You have no way of knowing" statement on me. I was in the Army, sitting in the back of a "deuce-and-a-half" truck, along with several other transfer soldiers, being transported to our new assigned post in West Germany. Across from me sat a black GI who mentioned that he was from Detroit. Naturally, I piped in that I, too, hailed from Detroit. "Oh yeah, where abouts?," he asked. When I told him that I actually lived in one of the neighboring suburbs of Detroit, he was quick to remind me that suburban life was not at all the same thing as living in the inner-city. Of course, I understood his point, but what was lost in our introduction was any semblance that we shared *anything* in common because we technically grew up 11 miles apart. Such are the unfortunate racial barriers that we ourselves choose to build, which only stifle any hope of finding whatever commonalities exist between the races.

Perhaps the most intelligent argument I ever heard concerning racial and ethnic equality came from the most unlikely of sources - my Drill Sergeant from Basic Training, whose last name was Custer (if you can believe it). It was 1971, the military draft was starting to wind down, so we had a complete potpourri of trainees of every color, religion, and ethnic group, all being verbally abused, equally, by Drill Sergeant Custer. One night, in the barracks, Custer had to jump in to break up a fight between two trainees, one who was black and the other one white. He threw the two GIs on the barracks floor, stood over them like Muhammad Ali over a knocked-out Sonny Liston, and proceeded to read them the Riot Act. That "Riot Act" ended up completely shattering any notion that anyone of us might have previously held that we were anything other than one band of brothers.

Drill Sergeant Custer was an Airborne Infantryman who had served multiple tours of Vietnam during the 1960s. Over our 8 weeks of training, when he wasn't demonstrating the proper way to withdraw one's bayonet from the body of a dead Vietcong soldier, Custer would sometimes sit in the barracks with his men and share some of his experiences "in the bush." But today, poised over the prostrated bodies of two frightened GIs, surrounded by a captive audience of the rest of Third Platoon, he was to take on a new role - that of a wise old sage - and we were about to get the ultimate sermon on racial equality.

Custer ordered the two men to get on their feet and snap to attention, which they did immediately. He then circled around the two men like a hungry panther considering his prey. After several rotations of scrutiny, Custer stopped in front of the black trainee, grabbed the dog tags hanging around his neck, and read what was written on them. In a booming voice, he read the GI's name, ID number, blood type, and religion. Releasing the chain, he then stepped in front of the white GI, grabbed his dog tags, and read the information stamped upon them. Custer then let go of the chain, told the two trainees to stand at ease, then slowly turned around and faced the rest of Third Platoon.

"What did you just learn about these two men?," he asked. "The United States Army has gone through the trouble of summarizing everything they feel is important about you, on a one-by-two inch stainless steel oval, stamped with only that information I just read to you. What does it say about you as a soldier? I'll tell you. Your name and military ID number is only on there so we know whose body we're shipping back home should you be killed on the field of battle. Your blood type is on there so that, if your guts are oozing through your fingers on that field of battle, that we can match you up with another GI for a transfusion that might save your life. And, believe me, if half your guts are lying in your lap, you're not going to care if that transfusion is coming from a GI who's black, white, Jewish, Christian, Italian or Hispanic. And your religion is only listed on there so that we can find an appropriate chaplain to pray over your body should you be killed in combat." At that, Custer paused, and began to walk around the room, staring into the faces of his men.

"That's why the United States Army puts that specific information on your dog tags," Custer continued. "But what does that same information say about you as a man, as a human being? I'll tell you. Your name and ID number only describe who you are in this world, *externally*. A name and a number tells you absolutely nothing about who you are *inside*. Naturally, the type of blood that is pumped through your body by your heart, and runs through every vein in your body, defines the *internal* physical miracle of who you are *inside*. And your religion? Well, that defines who you are, *internally*, as a child of God." At that, Custer paused again, and returned to the two GIs who had been fighting.

"I don't ever want to see this type of behavior in my barracks again," he said forcibly. "Whether you die in some rice paddy in 'Nam, or in your sleep at the age of 90, you had better figure out that the only important thing about you is who you are inside. You are all created in the image of God, every single one of you. That is the only truth you need to carry forward through life, however short or long that may be." With that, Drill Sergeant Custer turned and headed for the door. "Reveille is at 0400," were the last words he said as he exited the barracks.

* * *

At 0400 the following morning, I was awakened by the startling shock of all the fluorescent ceiling lights being switched on, along with the sound of our Assistant Drill Sergeant yelling, at the top of his booming voice, "Alright ladies, time to drop your c**ks and grab your socks. Get out of bed, my little darlings. Your mommies aren't here to make you Mickey Mouse waffles for breakfast, but I'm here to bust your asses at PT this morning. So get the f*ck out of those bunks, now!" As I slowly returned to consciousness, I suddenly realized that Drill Sergeant Custer wasn't the one waking us up this morning – and that was because he had been sick with pneumonia for the past four days.

It had all been a dream, all of it. As I slowly made my way to the latrine, to brush my teeth, my eyes only half open, I thought about what was said by Sergeant Custer in my dream. As I brushed my teeth, I looked into the mirror and slowly began to realize that, just because what I dreamt that night never really happened, it didn't mean that Custer's words, within my dream, weren't absolutely true. Because they were! The truth of his words, although only "heard" in the unconscious mind of an 18-year-old soldier, has stayed with me ever since.

Perhaps that one particular dream best explains how, oftentimes, even our unconscious selves can still "hear" God speak to our souls. I certainly try to consciously keep my ears ever open for God's gentle whisper, and He certainly does speak to my inner Being, because that is where He resides. In other words, God's words of truth come to us, irrespective of time or space, to guide us forward, even in our dreams.

This is just as it was the night He appeared to me, dressed as an Army Staff Sergeant by the name of Custer. And He told me that all men are created equal, so I had better treat them that way. How very like God to see to it that I would learn the truth about racial equality - by having a dream about racial equality.

CHAPTER 3

CONSCIOUSNESS (AWARENESS)

With all your science can you tell how it is, and
whence it is, that light comes into the soul?
- Henry David Thoreau

A Journey To The Center

B eneath a clear, diamond-studded celestial canopy, three score noble silence practitioners are assembled within the sanctuary of an oceanfront shala, for our pre-dawn vipassana meditation. Before closing my eyes, I observe how completely enveloping the darkness is that surrounds us - there is absolutely nothing visibly distinguishable beyond the perimeter of our huge tent. The only discernible sound is the ocean's waves breaking on the nearby rocky shore. The early morning chill is the primary exterior sensation my body feels as I proceed inward, to center.

I breathe deeply into my center point, my *dan t'ien*, my lower belly. [In Reginald A. Ray's *The Awakening Body* (2016), we learn that Taoists consider this special somatic space as "the inner expression of the fundamental space of the cosmos, the original womb out of which all energy and life arise. . . . By tapping into the lower dan t'ien, we are able to tap into the primal, unformed energy of the universe itself."[27]] Since thoughts tend to draw our attention away from what we're actually feeling, I try not to think during vipassana meditation. Because sensations are where the mind and body meet, rather than focusing on (i.e. thinking about) the flow of my breath, I simply try to *feel* the sensation of my nostrils expanding and contracting with each breath, and the soft movement of my nostril hairs while breathing.

The primary goal of vipassana is cultivating awareness and equanimity. It is believed by many that vipassana is the method of meditation the Buddha himself practiced and taught to others. It centers on having a detached mind, to completely accept what is, and to just *be.* According to the Buddha, "Everything that arises in the mind flows together with sensations."[28] True peace of mind befalls he who simply focuses on impermanent sensations - they are the link between the physical and the mental. The mind and body are inseparable and, therefore, nondualistic in nature.

Having my eyes closed during meditation only enhances my other senses of hearing, touch, and smell. The soft sound of the waves on the beach is soothing to my ears, and the gentle ocean breeze blows cool upon my face and hair. Suddenly, the stillness of the morning is broken by the sounds of the first awakening mynas, welcoming the new day from the large banyan tree behind our shala. Within seconds, there is a cacophony of other mynas responding to nature's morning reveille call. I welcome these new sounds and try to convey them into my memory bank.

Moments later, I begin to breathe in the first heavenly aromas coming from MaryAnn's kitchen, a prelude to the sumptuous vegan feast which we all will be enjoying within the hour - our healthy "morning fuel" as she likes to call breakfast. Simply inhaling the savory smells, carried by the early morning breeze, through my nostrils, and deeply into my body, fills me with a delightful anticipation. In fact, I can almost *taste* the food behind the smell - such is its appetizing appeal. As much as I try to only *feel* the sensation of smell, without *thinking* about the food responsible for the smell, I find myself conceptualizing the preparation of this food, cooked with lovingkindness by MaryAnn.

I cannot resist the temptation to slowly open my eyes, just enough to see the first vestige of daylight, revealing the silhouettes of the surrounding trees and nearby island. I glance about me, to see the other 60 spiritual pilgrims inside the shala, sitting cross-legged and completely motionless. I can't help but feel like the lone space traveler on an intergalactic starship, who's hibernation pod has prematurely opened, and now finds himself surrounded by his fellow cosmic voyagers, all sleeping within the innermost depths of their beings. As both of my feet are noticeably asleep, I very slowly begin to extend my legs, while keeping an eye on our leader as if he were a prison guard, and I an escaping inmate. Seeing everyone else in perfect meditation poses, so still, and assumedly *centered*, I suddenly feel like the only student in gym class who can't do a proper chin-up.

But what I suddenly realize is that I have now, literally, become The (External) Observer - that person everyone else is attempting to become, internally, within his or her meditation practice. Very quietly, and ever so slowly, I lengthen my legs and lean back upon my elbows (while still keeping our leader in view out of the corner of my eye). No longer am I focused on breathing deeply into my *dan t'ien*, that special spot believed to be three finger lengths below, and two finger widths behind, the navel. Personally, it is enough for me to know that my center point, my conscious center, is *somewhere* inside of me. ("Close enough for government work," as we used to say in the Army). I mean, after all, when Jesus said that The Kingdom of God is within us, He didn't feel a need to specify that it was located exactly so many inches from our liver or spleen.

Ever so slowly, the dark silhouetted trees begin to display their true colors of greens and browns, the distant island rises above a deep blue ocean, and the morning sky displays the light pink and purple hues of dawn. I am one with everything I see before me, and I breathe all of it into my inner being, my center. All that I am resides there. Every single sight, sound, and smell that I am experiencing during this lovely early morning meditation is being deposited into the treasure trove of my conscious center.

After an entire lifetime of looking "out there" for God, Truth, Love, Happiness and Knowledge, I now know that all of the most elusive, sought-after answers to life already lie within me - and they always have. This morning's awakening has become my awakening. By being acutely conscious of the genesis of this new day, I allow all of my sensations to synthesize within me, so as to become one with my being, my center, my soul. For it is within this eternal depository that this dawn will live forever - long after I have taken my last mortal breath.

If I learned anything from my 10-day vipassana experience, it was exactly what Dr. Jordan B. Peterson noted in *12 Rules For Life* (2018): "There is no enlightened one. There is only the one who is seeking further enlightenment. Proper Being is process, not a state; a journey, not a destination. It's the continual transformation of what you know, through encounter with what you don't know, rather than the desperate clinging to the certainty that is eternally insufficient in any case."[29]

Picking Up The Pieces

Happy New Year!

No single day of the year seems to possess the same degree of promise, and hopeful aspirations, as does New Year's Day. No matter how many of the previous year's resolutions we have broken, or entirely forgot about, this year will always be different, right? How do we know that? Because we only made these new resolutions five minutes ago, and still believe that we have it within us to see them through (with any luck, at least to February). If you don't believe that this is common to most people, check out the statistics of how many gym memberships are started in January, and then cancelled within the next three months.

My "problem" is this: three years ago, I made a list of **permanent** resolutions that I vowed never to renege on. What I did was to take my daily "To Do" List (something that I never strictly adhered to) and started to call it a "Must Do" List. I know what you're thinking. Who would do such a remarkably stupid thing? Well, I did. And, of course, the next question is, Why would you want to do such a dumb thing as that? I guess my initial reason was because, after six decades, I was simply tired of making daily (and annual) resolutions which, for the most part, I never followed through with. But the main reason for creating a "Must Do" List was because I was finally willing to commit, wholeheartedly, to a philosophy of daily living which I had created for myself - something I call *The Pono Principle* (Balboa Press, 2017).

Simply stated, *Pono* is the Hawaiian philosophy of doing the right thing in all areas of one's life. In my book, I share personal stories from my life, reflecting on how "doing the right thing" has always been the ultimate answer to any life challenge I have ever faced. At the end of every chapter, I share a life lesson that, oftentimes, reveals where I have completely failed to practice pono myself (in a certain situation), or how difficult it has been for me to adhere to *The Pono Principle* on a daily basis. These life lessons are but mere reminders to the reader that "living pono" is a practice based on progress, not perfection.

One of the life lessons I discuss in *The Pono Principle* has to do with my morning beachwalks in Wailea, where I live. For far too many years (i.e. most of my life), I was the type of individual who would never have thought about picking up litter which I hadn't discarded myself. Somewhere, within my rationalizing brain, I would make the case that it wasn't my responsibility to clean up after other litterbugs - let "someone else" deal with it, I would think. (It's difficult for me to write these words right now, such is my guilt). But, then a miracle happened.

One morning, while taking my beachwalk, I not only thought about picking up someone else's discarded cigarette butt - I even made a conscious decision to pick it up - and then, most importantly, I took the necessary pono action step by actually picking it up and carrying it to the nearest garbage receptacle. This was a life changing moment in time for me. It is true to say that, because I was writing a book at the time about doing the right thing in all things (i.e. Pono), I had a moment of clarity that literally stopped me in my tracks and beckoned me to pick up this one cigarette butt. It may have been my first enlightened moment of "other consciousness," a foreign concept to the person I was the day before.

But on this day, I chose to remove the blinders from my eyes - but not just to let God's light shine upon me. On this special morning, I allowed the light of God to shine from *within* me. And **that** is what has made all the difference in my life ever since. As a spiritual pilgrim, trying every day to follow the path God sets before me, I now try to look for every opportunity to get out of *my* self, and to be more conscious of others. Some may ask, "At the end of the day, what does one discarded cigarette butt mean to anyone?" (The "old" me would have very likely asked that question). What I learned that morning is that this is not *my* planet, it is *our* planet, and every single one of us bears a common responsibility to care for it.

* * *

So, guess what happened this morning? It's New Year's Day, and I'm taking my morning beachwalk in Wailea. At the very moment I arrive at the beach, and am about to head south on the sidewalk, I spot some broken glass on the ground. And I'm not talking about a small amount of glass here. Someone had obviously dropped a sizable glass bottle on the cement pathway, so there was glass everywhere - several large broken pieces, a lot of small pieces, and a million tiny shards. Of course, my first reaction was to look upward to the sky, and smile that acknowledging smile when I know that I just had a "God shot." It is also customary, when I hear God's gentle whisper, for me to drop to my knees. And so I did - as I began to pick up the shattered pieces of glass, scattered all about me, with my bare hands.

Kneeling on the pathway, picking up someone else's broken bottle, reminded me of the life lesson I had learned three years earlier, and related in *The Pono Principle*. I couldn't help to think that this was God's way of demonstrating to me that I need look no further than this broken bottle to find my New Year's resolution for today. Simply stated, He was telling me, "Robert, you don't need to ever make another resolution. Just practice the Pono Principle. After all, you wrote the book. Now, go live it every day."

And so I shall.

We Are The Light

I am the light of the world. - John 8:12
You are the light of the world. - Matt. 5:14 (NIV)

We are lost at sea - well, not exactly. The Captain has just made an announcement, over the intercom, giving us our latitudinal and longitudinal coordinates, so we're not, technically, "lost." Perhaps a better word would be *directionless*. That is to say, as of this moment in time, our ship (the MS *Westerdam*) doesn't have a defined port of call, or even a heading to guide us in any particular direction.

What was supposed to be a two-week Holland America cruise from Hong Kong to Shanghai has now morphed into "the cruise to nowhere" because of something called coronavirus disease (COVID-19). What started out as a localized virus in Wuhan, China, has now slowly spread to many other countries . . . and cruise ships. One such ship, the *Diamond Princess* is currently being quarantined in Yokohama, Japan, with several dozen passengers having tested positive for the disease. Currently, there are over 35,000 cases of coronavirus worldwide, and over 700 deaths.

This morning, I went to Mass and personally prayed for acceptance of our current situation. Together, with Father Robert and the rest of the congregation, we prayed for all those who have been affected by this thing called coronavirus. Father read from the Gospel according to Matthew, the passage commonly referred to as the Sermon on the Mount. Whereas, in several verses from John's Gospel, Jesus proclaims, "I am the light of the world," here in Matthew's Gospel, Jesus seems to be passing - or, better yet, sharing - the torch of His Divine Light to each of us, when He says, "You are the light of the world." That really stuck with me.

Father Robert followed the Gospel with a sermon focused on the Blessed Virgin Mary, referred to by sailors as the Star of the Sea. He asked us to consider how alike a twinkling star is to a lighthouse. The beaming light at the top of a lighthouse rotates somewhat slowly. But, from a distance, its light pierces the darkness very much like a twinkling star, only slower. To sailors, Mary represents the twinkling Star of the Sea that will guide them across stormy seas, or serve as their beacon when they are lost at sea.

Metaphorically, Mary is the guiding light to her Son, Jesus. Her entire *raison d'être* was not just to bring Jesus into this world - but, far more importantly, to bring the world to Him. From the first star that beckoned the three kings and the shepherds to Bethlehem, where Mary held her newborn Son in her arms, until the cross at Calvary, where Mary held the body of her crucified Son, she has always beckoned us to Him. Her eternal prayer seems to be that, by her guiding light, we may all come to discover the One who is truly "the light of the world."

But today's Gospel wasn't telling us to find the light within Jesus - it was Jesus telling us to find the light within ourselves. He tells us: "Let your light shine before others, that they may see your good deeds and glorify your Father in heaven."[30] (Matt. 5:16, NIV). Jesus is charging us with the task of demonstrating goodness to others in everything we do. In that way, we shine "our light" throughout the world, thereby glorifying God at the same time. This is the ultimate win-win-win outcome (what I call The Pono Principle).

By no coincidence, today's 1st Reading from the Book of Isaiah spoke exactly to that: "Deal thy bread to the hungry, and bring the needy and the harbourless into thy house: when thou shalt see one naked, cover him, and despise not thy own flesh. Then shall thy light break forth as the morning."[31] (Isaiah 58:7-8, DRC). The fact that this Reading actually used the word *harbourless* is astounding to me, for that is exactly what we are at this time, a ship without a harbour (or even a destination, for that matter). It also spoke to the very real need to care for one another as we, collectively, continue on this "cruise to nowhere." Not everyone is as "accepting" of our current situation as I may be. Which got me to thinking: What can I do to possibly relieve the tension some of my fellow passengers may be experiencing right now?

Recently, I wrote to the Captain, explaining that I was the author of *The Pono Principle*, a book about doing the right thing in all situations, and that I had a Master's Degree in Human Services Counseling: Life Coaching. I told him that I would be happy, and honored, to volunteer to speak to the passengers and crew of the *Westerdam* on the subject of *Acceptance*, should he find that service of value. Those of us in addiction recovery know fully well that acceptance is the foundation upon which sincere, lifelong sobriety is built. Considering the day-to-day uncertainty of our ship's next move, it is no surprise to me that I haven't heard back from the Captain. To suggest that he is knee-deep in alligators right now would be a gross understatement.

My takeaway from today's Mass is that I am still a light to shine for others, regardless of how many (or how few) are within its rays. All I have the ability to do, right now, at this moment, is to offer myself to those who need to be comforted, or just listened to. To whom may I be a light today? Perhaps to my dining room table neighbors, who are older than I, and less accepting of our current circumstances than I. Perhaps to our recovery group that will be meeting later today, who might be tempted to drink during this stressful time we are experiencing. Perhaps the best that I can do today is to politely greet every person I walk by, just as an assurance that, together, we will get through this.

There is a port awaiting us, although we see it not at this

moment. There is a star waiting to guide us, a lighthouse to show us the way, and a harbour to welcome us home. Until such time, we must be a light for each other, and enfold our arms around one another - in the same way Mary held her child, beneath a star, a star that guided all of humanity to its light.

The Icon of Full Consciousness

The ultimate goal in Buddhism is to reach the transcendent state of nirvana, an enlightened mental state of perfect peace and happiness. Those who have achieved nirvana become free of (i.e. transcend) human suffering and bad karma. In the Christian faith, many would say that the ultimate goal is for one's soul to go to Heaven when one dies. Certainly, that may be a Christian's "eternal" goal, in the afterlife, but while we are still living within these mortal bodies, the most important thing a Christian desires is to become God-conscious and Christ-centered. The Incarnation of Jesus made it possible for believers to connect to God the Father, and to become fully conscious of God the Father, in a way never before experienced – and *only* by becoming fully conscious of God the Son. To become *fully conscious* of Jesus Christ is, indeed, the very essence of salvation. In Fr. Richard Rohr's *Immortal Diamond* (2013), the Franciscan priest observes:

> You cannot build any serious spiritual house if you do
> not first find something solid and foundational to build
> on - inside yourself. 'Like knows like' is the principle.
> God-in-you already knows, loves, and serves God and
> everything else. All you can do is fully jump on board.
> I would call that jump consciousness, and I believe the
> Risen Christ is the icon of full consciousness. In the
> human mind of Christ, every part of creation knows
> itself as (1) divinely conceived, (2) beloved of God, (3)

crucified, and (4) finally reborn. He carries us across
with him, assures us it is okay, and thus models the full
journey and final direction of consciousness. That is
my major thesis about how Jesus 'saves us.'[32]

Consciousness and Being

Each of us tries to be conscious of everything that is happening to us, around us, and within us, at all times. What so many people associate with the workings of their physical, mortal *bodies*, especially their thoughts and feelings, has little (if anything) to do not with defining their inner *Beings*. Our thoughts and feelings are merely things we observe. But how can we *be* that which we observe? The answer is: our true Being is something much, much, bigger. According to Ken Wilber, in *The Simple Feeling of Being* (2004), "You are that Witness, aren't you? You are the pure Seer, pure awareness, the pure Spirit that impartially witnesses everything that arises, moment to moment. . . . That very Witness is Spirit within, looking out on a world that it created."[33]

Only when individuals ascend to a level of consciousness where they are completely aware that they are not (and never have been) the actor on stage – but, instead, the eyes that are observing the actor on stage - can they begin to understand the true breadth of their Being. One's true Spirit *is* the Witness, the Divine Self, which oversees, but is not the physical body of that unenlightened Ego Self who goes around town using your name. Returning to Ken Wilber, in his book *One Taste* (1999), the author states:

> *So what do I see? If I contract as ego, it appears that*
> *I am confined in the body, which is confined in the*
> *house, which is confined in the large universe around*
> *it. But if I rest as the Witness - the vast, open, empty,*
> *consciousness - it becomes obvious that I am not in*

> the body, the body is in me; I am not in this house, the
> house is in me; I am not in the universe, the universe is
> in me. All of them are arising in the vast, open, empty,
> pure, luminous Space of primordial Consciousness,
> right now and right now and forever right now.
> Therefore, be Consciousness.[34]

CHAPTER 4

HAPPINESS (JOY)

Happiness depends more on the inward disposition of
mind than on outward circumstances.
- Benjamin Franklin

How often in life have we said (or heard others say), "If I had *only* done this or that, I would have been happy," or "If I could *only* move here or there, I'd be happy," or "If I *only* had more money, I'd be happy?" It seems to be part of humanity's DNA to second-guess how much happier we would be if we *only* made different past, present, or future choices in life. We seem to live under the delusion that happiness only comes to us, externally, when we change our circumstances, or when our circumstances improve.

My dear gypsy mother, God rest her soul, lived a lifetime seeking happiness somewhere on the distant horizon, where she was confident that the grass was always greener. Every geographic move we made as a family, during my youth, was merely a means of satisfying my mother's wanderlust and search for a happier life. Even though she possessed a joyful spirit, and a cheerful persona, I do believe that she thought there was some sort of treasure trove of happiness waiting for her, just over the next hill, if she were just willing to go and get it. I wish my mother had read Richard Bach's *Illusions* (1977) where the "Reluctant Messiah" observes, "For the love of God, if you want freedom and joy so much, can't you see it's not anywhere outside of you? Say you have it, and you have it! Act as if it's yours, and it is!"[35]

Being my mother's son, I inherited her gypsy blood, but I'm not so sure that happiness was my ultimate goal every time I made a major move somewhere. For me, personally, I think I had a thirst for adventure more than anything else. I certainly never thought that whatever change I was bringing into my life would *make* me happy, probably because I have always felt that there already was a reservoir of happiness within my soul - it was just up to me to tap into it.

We've all heard people say that they have a "happy place" where they like to go to de-stress, relax, and enjoy themselves. It usually implies some form of sanctuary where one can escape the rat race of everyday life. Perhaps Disneyland (the self-proclaimed "Happiest Place On Earth") exemplifies that quality to children and adults alike, because it harkens back to pleasing memories of Disney movies and characters from the more innocent days of our youth. A spa resort, a desert island, or mountain retreat might be other examples of geographic "happy places" people seek when the stormy winds of life are too much for them.

Ironically, even the most powerful, violent storms on earth - Category 5 hurricanes - have a clear, calm center at their core. If the Greater Los Angeles area can be looked at as the paragon of rat race stress and anxiety, Disneyland is that calm, peaceful oasis at its center. It represents the ideal haven for anyone trying to find a "happy place" to escape to. But, as we all eventually discover, true happiness is not to be found in an external destination - whether Disneyland, Bora Bora, or that imaginary Shangri-La over the next hill.

Then what is happiness? It is a feeling, a state of mind, an internal sense of peace, joy and well-being. But, where does it come from, and where does it exist? Does it exist for everyone? Can it be shared with others, or is it a unique sensation for each individual? Can happiness be summoned at will? If so, how?

This past year, I became a grandparent for the seventh time. The sheer jubilation and happiness I felt the day I received the news of another grandchild, completely filled me with joy that entire day. But, did I still feel the same amount of elation the following day, or a week later? Did the degree of my happiness, as a result of that birth *event*, wane over time? Is it possible it could ever disappear altogether? Not if I carefully, and faithfully, store it within the safe depository of my inner Being - for that is where my true happiness ultimately resides.

The big question becomes: How often do I choose to *visit* the happiness that lives within me? Many people go through life looking for that next *thing* to *make* them happy, without ever thinking to resource what is so readily accessible to them - not "out there" - but internally. The quickest way to an unhappy existence is to become dependent upon other people, things, events, or outcomes - expecting *them* to *make* you happy. The elation one feels after winning a football game won't carry you through a subsequent losing streak unless you can *replay* that one victory in your mind, vividly, long enough for you to, once again, feel happy about it. Football games, like political elections, are classic examples of how people (particularly those who depend on *outcomes* to make them happy) will either go home cheering at the top of their lungs, or will be completely devastated because of that one particular *event*. By their very nature, competitive events can never make both sides "happy." Therefore, my advice is to not take them so seriously.

Because I choose not to rely on external forces to bring happiness to my doorstep, I work at "self-generating" happiness - by living in the present moment, and by maintaining an attitude of gratitude. My own constructive thoughts and actions have generated much of the happiness I have known for the majority of my life. By simply reflecting on the most positive memories I have filed away, spanning a lifetime, I can instantly conjure up an inner peace, or a sense of joy, that otherwise would lie dormant and forgotten. Happiness is always there to be found - if I only look inside myself.

Because I was referencing Disneyland earlier, I couldn't help but smile as I remembered the many trips our family has taken, over the years, to most of the Disney theme parks (both in the U.S. and internationally). My memories of those trips, and how happy our children (and subsequent grandchildren) were every time we visited those Magic Kingdoms, still fills me with joy *today*. Such is the reward for preserving our memories of life's happiest moments.

I was just two years old when Disneyland opened in Anaheim, California, in July 1955. Since I grew up in Florida and Michigan, my parents never thought of California as a place to go on vacation. To their way of thinking, Los Angeles was on the other side of the earth, and the Golden Gate was just "a bridge too far." Consequently, they never took my younger brother and I to Disneyland (or to California for that matter). But something fortuitous occurred in 1971, the year I graduated from high school and enlisted in the U.S. Army - Disney World opened in Florida.

Just before I was transferred overseas, in March 1972, my gypsy mother decided that she was going to take my 10-year-old brother and me to Disney World, and stay at the Polynesian Village (one of only two hotels there at the time). Since none of us had ever been to Disneyland, our introduction to Disney World was filled with constant wonder and joy. I got to witness my mother as never before - laughing on the rides and making sure that we saw absolutely everything there was to see in the Magic Kingdom during the time we were there.

The three of us had the time of our lives on that trip together - but no one more than my mother. Having her two sons with her, in such a wondrous place, filled her with such a refreshing joy, and a deep-seated happiness, which I'm sure stayed in her heart forever. Witnessing the degree of my mother's joy *then* has only compounded the happy memories I have *now* of that trip we shared. And the only way I have of reliving that joy and happiness we felt those many years ago, is by going inside myself, to that sacred place where I can still see my 48-year-old mother - riding on Cinderella's Golden Carousel, or eating an ice cream cone on Main Street, U. S. A. - acting just like the happy little girl she once was many years earlier.

> *Preserve your memories, They're all that's left you.*
> - Paul Simon, *Bookends*

Joy does not come from what you do; it flows into what
you do and thus into this world from deep within you.
- Eckhart Tolle

Speaking of Children and Magic Kingdoms

My eldest grandson just turned nine recently, so I phoned him to wish him a Happy Birthday. During our conversation, I mentioned to him that I had often thought that the happiest time in my life was when I was nine years old. When he asked me why, I replied that it was a time in my life when I remember the unbridled freedom of riding my bicycle around my Miami neighborhood all summer long (and all day long if I wanted); building makeshift tree houses with my Cuban and Puerto Rican friends; discovering the joy of reading books, for the first time, at the public library; watching John Glenn, on our black-and-white television, as he orbited the earth in Friendship 7; and meeting New York Yankee Roger Maris, who signed a baseball for me at the Jordan Marsh department store on Biscayne Boulevard. It was a very innocent, yet magical, time in my life.

Reflecting back on those days of my youth makes me realize just how accurately Frederick Buechner describes the very essence of childhood innocence and awareness in *The Magnificent Defeat* (1966):

> *Jesus says that in order to enter the kingdom of Heaven*
> *we must become like children, and this gives rise to the*
> *most poignant kind of awareness of how we ourselves*
> *were children once but are no longer, of the dreaming*
> *innocence we lost without ever intending to lose it, of*
> *a summery, green world where everything was possible,*
> *where in the end the evil dragon was always slain and*
> *the princess rescued from her tower - all of this replaced*

> now by a winter world about which we feel that we
> know far too much, a world where again and again we
> see ourselves as not least among the dragons.[36]

But how can we - how do we - return to that innocent time in our lives, when we were our happiest and most joyful selves? How do we "change and become like little children" so as to be called "the greatest in the kingdom of Heaven?" Buechner answers that question thusly:

> It is just when we realize that it is impossible by any
> effort of our own to make ourselves children and
> thus to enter the kingdom of Heaven that we become
> children. We are children, perhaps, at the very moment
> when we know that it is as children that God loves
> us - not because we have deserved his love and not
> in spite of our underserving; not because we try and
> not because we recognize the futility of our trying;
> but simply because he has chosen to love us. We are
> children because he is our father; and all our efforts,
> fruitful and fruitless, to do good, to speak truth, to
> understand, are the efforts of children who, for all their
> precocity, are children still in that before we loved him,
> he loved us, as children, through
> Jesus Christ our Lord.[37]

In Search of a Happy Life

In his *Confessions*, St. Augustine equates his search for God with having a happy life: "Let me seek you so that my soul can live: my body lives from my soul, and my soul lives from you. So how do I seek a happy life? - because I don't have it until I can say, 'Fine: it's there.'[38]" What Augustine means by "there" is within one's self – that is, within one's memory. He states, "A happy life isn't seen with the eyes, because it's not a physical thing.[39]" He is basically concluding that a "happy life" cannot be found anywhere "out there;" happiness and joy only exist when remembered:

> *I remember my joy even when I'm sad, as a miserable*
> *man remembers a happy life, but I never saw or heard*
> *or smelled or tasted or touched my joy through physical*
> *perception; instead I felt it in my mind at the time I*
> *was made glad, and the knowledge of*
> *it clung to my memory.*[40]

But Augustine firmly declares that his true joy, and happy life, comes only through his relationship with God. He says, "This is happy life itself: to rejoice in your presence, and through you, and because of you. This life is the actual happy life; there is no other kind. Those who think the happy life is different pursue another joy, and not the true one itself."[41]

A Profile In Happiness and Joy
- Sarah Taylor, MS, MBA

In 2002, Sarah Taylor read John Robbins' *Diet for a New America*, thinking that it was a weight-loss book – she became a vegan instead. That was a very transformative moment for the 30-year-old woman from Gig Harbor, Washington. According to Sarah, Robbins' book "not only turned me vegan overnight, but also set me on a spiritual trajectory that has changed my life forever." Over the ensuing years, Sarah has, herself, authored two books about veganism, one entitled *Vegan in 30 Days* (2008), the other *Vegetarian to Vegan* (2013). She has an MBA in Research Methodologies from Seattle University, as well as a Certificate in Plant Based Nutrition from Cornell University. Sarah was also on faculty at the Nutritional Education Institute, where she worked as a Motivational Trainer for Joel Fuhrman, MD, the NY Times best-selling author of *Eat to Live*.

In addition to her life-changing transition to a healthy vegan diet, Sarah also enjoys playing tennis, scuba diving, studying spirituality and adventure traveling. Sarah and her husband, Mark, began to come to Maui a little over a decade ago. It was about that time that she started to meditate and doing kirtan chants. She started to experience different religions, not just read about them. Everything in her head started to move down to her heart. In 2011, on one of their many visits to Maui, Sarah and Mark decided to come to the financial aid of the Leilani Farm Sanctuary in Haiku, an island treasure.

I first met Sarah, some years ago, during a yoga class at the Wailea Healing Center. My yoga instructor introduced us and suggested that I read Sarah's books on veganism. I remember her having a very cheerful demeanor and positive presence. It was only recently that I learned that Sarah had been diagnosed with Glioblastoma - Stage 4 brain cancer. Since I knew that she and Mark were here on Maui, I called her and asked if she would be willing to do an interview. She kindly accepted my invitation.

By this time, Sarah had already posted several updates on her condition on social media, and I also watched interviews she had done for two separate podcasts. What was consistent throughout every post and interview was Sarah's genuinely positive perspective - one of uplifting optimism, gratitude, and light. Her message is one of acceptance, and she maintains that at no time since her diagnosis has she been upset. She credits her spirituality for preparing her for such an unexpected turn of events. What healthy 48-year-old woman expects to be told, out of the blue, that she has Stage 4 brain cancer?

When I asked Sarah that question, she responded, "If I had had this diagnosis 15 years ago, I would probably be like the average person - fearful, crying, saying 'Oh my God, my poor husband,' or

'Oh, this is terrible' - it would have been very average, I think. But having gone through all this, I've just come up with my own beliefs about who we are, why we're here, and whether we come back in the next life." Instead, Sarah has reached a state of consciousness where she has come to accept that "whatever happens, it's okay." But, what spiritual pathway brought her to this level of acceptance?

In 2018, Sarah left a 20-year career in medical research with the hopes of making a bigger difference in people's lives through the counseling field. She received a Master's Degree in Mental Health Counseling from the University of Massachusetts, Boston. As part of her degree, Sarah completed her yearlong internship at the Washington Corrections Center for Women (the state women's prison). She then helped other people achieve balance and strength through a holistic lifestyle, treating adult individuals who were going through existential crises. Her main area of specialization was with cancer patients.

One of the existential exercises Sarah uses with her cancer patients is to have them imagine a roulette wheel – one that has red and black slots for every human being on earth that will live a long life - and ask these patients if they would be willing to roll the ball and then switch lives with the person whose slot the ball lands on. This was Sarah's way of counseling her patients on how to appreciate the life they've been given, both the good times and bad. That no matter how challenging their cancer experience might be, would they really want to swap their life for the life of a complete stranger? What about the stranger's unknown history? Their pain and suffering? Their life challenges? According to Sarah, she never once had a patient who wanted to risk switching their life for anyone else's, no matter how long they lived.

This past New Year's Eve, Sarah shared (on social media) her favorite quote which she had read in Paramahansa Yogananda's *Autobiography of a Yogi* (1946). The quote is attributed to Charles Robert Richet, a Nobel Prize winner in physiology, who declared, "It is assumed that the phenomena which we now accept without surprise, do not excite our astonishment because they are understood. But this is not the case. If they do not surprise us, it is not because they are understood, it is because they are familiar; for if that which is not understood ought to surprise us, we should be surprised at everything."[42]

For Sarah, this particular quote took on a whole new meaning when she substituted the word *apple* for *phenomena*. In a moment of enlightenment, she came to the realization that apples are merely familiar objects, and that she didn't truly *understand* the entire composition of an apple (i.e. how it is what it is). What is an apple's molecular, and chemical, makeup? How does its composition of nutrients benefit humans? Why does an apple taste the way it does? Never again would an "everyday" apple fail to fill Sarah with newfound anticipation and wonder. She would, forevermore, *experience* an apple as if for the very first time.

In truth, Sarah has never again looked upon anything around her as *familiar*. Like a modern-day Eve, taking her first stroll through the Garden of Eden, she now exists in a world where she lives in constant amazement of God's creative handiwork. Today, she will see the entire circle of life represented in a single leaf, just by taking the time to carefully contemplate it. When she sits with her 10-year-old cat (whose name she frequently forgets these days), she sits in wonder of the cat's paw and the softness of its hair. At this precious moment in her life, Sarah has come to understand that we must all slow down so as to be present for these moments of discovery and wonder. Because of her careful examination, and profound appreciation, of what is *familiar* to most, Sarah now marvels at the sound of the breeze as it blows through the leaves, and the gentle purring of her cat, and says, "I honor it all."

Living in the present moment is one of the two most profound life lessons Sarah has learned on her life journey - the other is to live in a perpetual state of gratitude. In the midst of dealing with a brain tumor that has caused her to lose some of her memory and, oftentimes in conversation, many common words, Sarah has also had to deal with hair loss from her chemo/radiation treatments, and her own self-assessment that she's "not smart anymore." And yet, when she so candidly discusses her current health challenges, she maintains a very cheerful, and positive demeanor. How, you may wonder?

Sarah is quick to respond that "we are not our bodies; we're not what we look like." If she has learned anything through this trying time, it is that "who" she truly is has absolutely nothing to do with her name, age, body, mind, or personality. None of those societal identifiers define her inner being, her soul. The answer to "who" Sarah is can best be witnessed by observing the level of acceptance she has in dealing with her cancer. "I don't want to go right now," she admits, "but I'm okay with it." For a 48-year-old woman to face her mortality so courageously, and with such grace, is an inspiration to everyone she has touched over these past months of her living with the uncertain threat of Stage 4 brain cancer. And the light that shines from within Sarah is one born out of joy and gratitude.

Sarah shared with me her "secret" to staying so upbeat and happy during this time in her life. "There are certain things in life that make us happy," she told me. "Who do we spend our time with? What do we do with our time? And where do we live?" Sarah suggests that a happy life is spent being around the people whose company you enjoy most – one's spouse, loved ones and friends. Enjoying one's chosen career is huge, especially if you can make a profession out of service to others. Lastly, choosing to live in an environment suited to your personal tastes will only make your life that much more joyful.

And, when (not if) life throws you a curveball - like divorce, getting fired from a job, or having brain cancer - may you find the grace and light of such a one as Sarah Taylor.

CHAPTER 5

PEACE (SERENITY)

*There can be no peace without, but through peace
within. Society must be an expression of
the souls of its members.*
— William E. Channing

World Peace Begins With Inner Peace

*Let There Be Peace on Earth And
Let It Begin with Me.*
- Jill Jackson & Sy Miller

The oldest stereotype concerning beauty pageants may be the number of times that contestants have answered "World peace" when asked what it is that they most hope for with regards to the future of our planet. The sentiment, however sincere (or feigned) it may be for each contestant, seems to always impress the judges. And, now that the bathing suit competition has been eliminated from all future pageants, the "World peace" interview response may be the only thing that impresses the judges. World peace may, in fact, be the noblest prayer known to humankind. But what kind of peaceful civilization can we expect to find in a world where there is less peace, and less civility, shown to others, than at any time in recent memory?

Perhaps the most obvious example that we see in our country today is the complete lack of civility shown to our fellow countrymen whose political views differ from our own. The vitriolic name-calling, and dismissive intolerance, demonstrated in political "discourse" is disgusting at best, and societally destructive at worst. Forget how our country's forefathers would react to this kind of "uncivil war" that exists today. I am just grateful that my own father isn't alive to witness what has happened to America, and its people - the two most honorable purposes for which he fought in World War Two.

Perhaps the saddest realization is that the very people spewing endless hateful epithets at others feel completely justified in doing so. They sanctimoniously identify "lesser" humans to verbally attack - a political figure, a corporation, a religious group - and can only feel superior to such others by dehumanizing and debasing them. It's what the Nazis did in the 1930s and '40s. It was the only way that Adolf Hitler could possibly rally so many fellow Germans to do what they did during those years. He had to convince his countrymen that certain ethnic and religious groups, and other nations, were to blame for all of Germany's woes. For the most part, Hitler succeeded in the effectiveness of his propaganda - and the world was never the same again.

What I find most ironic, today, is how similar the propaganda machine works within our current political arena. Whether the hateful messaging is coming from a Hitler-like leader (fill in your favorite hate-spewing politician's name here), to a Goebbels-like minister of propaganda (fill in your favorite hate-spewing media outlet here), the end result is the same: certain citizens will buy into the hate-messaging, drink the Kool-Aid, then hit the streets. What the Nazis of the '30s and '40s never understood was that **they** were the ones reeking havoc on the world - not the Jews, not the homosexuals, not America, nor the other European countries. One hateful man, successfully spreading his hateful ideas to others, is what destroyed world peace almost 80 years ago.

Likewise, in America today, it is the hate-spewing politicians, and their Kool-Aid drinking followers, who are disrupting both peace around the world and within our own communities. I have no doubt whatsoever that the vast majority of people around the world share a common maxim - Live and Let Live. Therefore, I do not believe that the masses bear responsibility for the political and social unrest we see plastered on the front pages of our daily newspapers. Most people wish to live in a peaceful world. Does anyone seriously doubt that, if given the freedom to verbally state their preferences, that the North Korean people would resoundingly push for the denuclearization of their country so as to live in a peaceful and safe country? Only one individual, Kim Jong-un, holds the power to make that dream a reality for the North Korean people, and only he can, likewise, determine if his actions result in their complete obliteration. He is the problem, not his people.

Sri Swami Satchidananda once said, "The ultimate quest of the entire world is peace. Only in peace do we have joy."[43] He equates peace to light in the world. Without peace, the world is a very dark place. And in these dark times, when so many are spewing hatred towards each other, it is important to remember that many more seek the light of peace and joy. The invitation that Satchidananda often offered his followers was for them to walk around as "lit candles," so as to share their light with all the other "unlit candles" of the world:

> Only a candle that is lit and shining can give a little
> light to the other candles. If you simply sit there as an
> unlit candle and listen to hours and hours and hours
> of talk about light, you won't get lit. You have to come,
> touch the lamp, and get a spark before you get lit. That
> is the duty of a disciple. After having seen a lit candle
> you should go, bow down, and then get the touch.
> Once you have gotten that, you work on yourself,
> make your life brighter.[44]

Ask yourself, "Do I fill my head with peaceful and loving thoughts, or have I allowed my peace to be hijacked by others who wish me to adopt their political ideologies and hateful views?" "What am I going to do today to protect and defend my inner peace - at all costs?" "Am I an unlit candle, of no use in these dark times of political unrest, or am I that hopeful light that appears in the darkness, that knows inner peace and joy, and brings it to my fellow brothers and sisters?"

Please, light your candle - by focusing on the peace that exists within you - and then go and share that light with the rest of the world.

Passing The Torch Of Peace

How very blessed I am to be able to study yoga from someone who studied directly under Sri Swami Satchidananda for over 30 years – Meenakshi Angel Honig. Every time we finish our yoga sessions with Savasana, the relaxation pose, Angel always adds the spiritual reminder, "Bring the awareness to the peace within, and just rest in the sweet peace of your own true nature." What Angel is reminding her students is that peace resides "within" our "true nature." It's the type of statement that can easily be lost to someone who is not being truly present in the moment. So, if you are lying in Savasana pose, and thinking about what you need to pick up at Costco when you finish yoga class, you are missing a most important pearl of wisdom.

The Egoic Need To Be Right

There's nothing ego loves more than to be right, which makes it an important and satisfying attachment to practice letting go of.
- Dr. Wayne W. Dyer

Almost nothing in this world comes close to the importance people put on the notion of "being right." The conviction of one's beliefs, and the degree to which an individual will stand firm in those beliefs, can certainly be an admirable quality. But what happens when you have conflicting beliefs between parties whose convictions are adamantine? Well, things like World Wars come to mind, polarizing partisan politics, family feuds, and inane boxer/brief debates. Worse, what happens when emotions trump reason when it comes to expressing our opinions? In those situations, you can expect Jerry Springer melees on stage, mob violence in the streets, and vitriolic United States Congressional hearings.

So, how the hell did we ever get to a place where our opinions became so important that we would sacrifice, literally, anything and everything just to feel vindicated in those opinions? The short answer is: at some point in our lives we began to attach our opinions to our egos. The moment we completely self-identify with our beliefs, opinions and actions, is the moment when "being right" takes on a whole new importance in our lives. Regardless of how many times I am baited by self-opinionated zealots to "defend" my personal political or religious views, I refuse to bite. What I have often found to be the case with such people is not a sincere desire (on their part) to have an intellectual debate on issues, but rather to obdurately spew out a barrage of prepared talking points in an attempt to intimidate, and silence, the "opposing view."

For this type of individuals, *being right* is tantamount to standing on an Olympic podium, having a Gold Medal hung around their necks, while raising their middle fingers high in the air. For them, it is such an ego-satisfying achievement to "win" their arguments that they don't really care how many lies they have to tell, who they have to denigrate to make their point, or what is being said by the individual who is countering their position. They will do whatever is necessary to satisfy that insatiable egoic need to be right.

Now, here's a question for you: "Have you ever witnessed a humble person act in this way?" Of course not. By its very nature, humility demands that we not seek adoration for either our opinions or actions. A humble person would sooner smirk at someone's foolish statement than engage in a heated debate with the individual. A humble person certainly has personal opinions just like everyone else. The difference is that ego doesn't motivate this type of individual - a respect of other people's opinions does. Humble people usually aren't personally *invested* in their opinions to the same degree as egocentrics. They are more prone to listening to others instead of doing all the talking. For that very reason, people who practice humility are usually more open to rational arguments put to them, and more likely to amend their own opinions when they hear a sound argument politely offered.

I suppose the real question we must ask ourselves when we fall into the trap of "having to be right" is: "Do I want to be right, or do I want to be happy?" When you see two people, or two groups of people, in hot debate, screaming at each other at the top of their lungs, do you ever get any sense, at all, that these are "happy" people? Or are you witnessing people that are oftentimes emotionally out of control, and probably more inclined to spit in the face of their arguing opponent than give them a loving embrace after the debate is over? Think of the famous scene in the 1967 classic *Cool Hand Luke*, when the Captain hits Luke over the head with a blackjack billy club, knocking him to the ground, and then stating, "What we've got here is . . . failure to communicate."

In Jordan B. Peterson's *12 Rules For Life (2018)*, the University of Toronto professor and clinical psychologist offers this advice to married couples when they find themselves in the midst of a heated argument: "You must decide whether to insist upon the absolute correctness of your view, or to listen and negotiate. You don't get peace by being right. You just get to be right, while your partner gets to be wrong - defeated and wrong. Do that ten thousand times and your marriage will be over (or you will wish it was). To choose the alterative - to seek peace - you have to decide that you want the answer, more than you want to be right. That's the way out of the prison of your stubborn preconceptions. That's the prerequisite for negotiation."[45]

You know, there was a time in the not-so-distant past, when many an individual, debating any issue whatsoever, could feel "self-satisfied" in the knowledge that he/she was "right," and simply walk away from an argument when it got too heated. When did our egoic need to be right cause us to enter into a war of words with another person as though we were two gladiators in the Roman Coliseum - just so we can proclaim to the world (or, at least, to the person we're arguing against) that we had "won" an argument? Without wasting too much time trying to answer *when* that occurred, the important thing to recognize is that it *did* occur. I have little doubt that the increase in the human ego's obsession to be right, over the years, is directly proportionate to a steady increase in marital, relational and civil strife, not to mention an unprecedented degree of social intolerance towards the opposing views of our fellow human beings.

To add insult to injury, it also seems quite evident to me that most arguments debated today are usually between individuals who don't rationally debate topics as much as they regurgitate talking points put out on social media by spin doctors and political ideologues. Of course, the secret to using nothing but talking points to defend one's opinion is: when your talking points are challenged, or when you can't quite remember what they are, one can always default to the time-tested "last resort" of unleashing a diatribe of vitriolic epithets at his/her opponent. By demeaning another individual with a verbal barrage of insulting labels - "racist, Nazi, Fascist, homophobe, xenophobe, misogynist," *ad infinitum* - the dumbest debater in the world can, at least, walk away from an argument thinking, "Well, I sure told that idiot off!"

Oftentimes, in today's world, that's all it takes to be "right."

Ascension Suspension

Come, let us build ourselves a city, with a tower that
reaches to the heavens, so that we may make a name
for ourselves.
. . . But the Lord came down to see the city and the
tower the people were building.

- Genesis 11:4-5 (NIV)

It has been my personal experience that, every now and then, God likes to command my full attention. Far be it from me to ever question why God is compelled to do this; I'm sure He has good reasons to. Oftentimes, He does it quite subtly, using a gentle whisper. After all, this method proved to be His most effective way of getting Elijah's attention in the Old Testament. Because I have made a daily vow to try to keep my ears open to God's whispers, I don't quite understand why, sometimes, He feels it necessary to put on some big, dramatic, theatrical production - when a gentle whisper might have done just fine. Which brings me to my first tour of Vietnam.

No, not that kind of tour. The closest I ever came to Saigon (now Ho Chi Minh City), during the Vietnam War, was singing about it in cadence songs while marching around Ft. Knox, Kentucky, when I was going through U. S. Army Basic Training during the Fall of 1971. So, here I am, almost 50 years later, taking a bus tour through, what is now, a bustling metropolis of over 9 million people. After a visit to the former Presidential Palace (now known as Independence or Reunification Palace), with a stop at Notre Dame Cathedral and the Central Post Office, our bus dropped us off in front of the 68-floor Bitexco Financial Tower, the tallest building in the city. All of us were given the option of either going up to the Skydeck on the 49th Floor, or to use our time shopping in the surrounding stores and cafés. Not necessarily a big fan of tall skyscrapers, I still felt like I was being called to visit the Skydeck - so I did.

62

After paying for our entrance tickets, a group of us was escorted to the two elevators that were to take us on a very quick, 40-second ride up to the Skydeck, 584 feet above the ground. When the first elevator door opened, the operator directed nine of us to get into it. Just before the doors closed, two more people decided to join us, which made the compartment fairly snug. No one seemed to mind, as we were reminded by the operator, who stayed behind, that the trip would only last 40 seconds. The operator then pushed the button for the Skydeck, wished us well, and the eleven of us began our rapid ascent within the cramped quarters of our elevator compartment. Our ascent was monitored on a computer screen that displayed the floor numbers as they quickly changed over the next half minute. That's when it happened.

Just as we were nearing our destination (the Skydeck on the 49th Floor), the elevator suddenly jolted and shuddered, and then screeched to a complete stop. The computer screen displayed the number 47. There was an immediate look of shock on the faces of everyone within the tight confines of our common space. "Oh, my God!" "What just happened?" "That didn't sound good." It took a little bit of time for all of us to come to grips with the fact that we had just abruptly stopped before reaching our destination. That's when individuals began to offer up suggestions as to what we should do now. "Push the alarm button," someone said. So, I did. A voice came on the intercom, but was difficult to hear because of the elevator music playing overhead. I explained that the elevator had just stopped with a jolt, two floors below the Skydeck floor. The man at the other end said for us to stay calm, and that he would get back to us shortly.

Two things I failed to mention are that 1) all eleven of us were part of a cruise ship excursion, and 2) the Tet Holiday (i.e. the Vietnamese Lunar New Year) was to occur in two days. In other words, most locals were more focused on the following day's New Year's Eve celebrations than on working. This fact begged the question, "Who's going to rescue us, and how long is that going to take? We have a two-hour bus ride back to our ship." After what seemed like an eternity, the voice came back on the intercom. When I told the man that it was hard to hear him, he informed us that he didn't have the ability to turn off the overhead music. All he basically told us was that they had people working on getting us out of the elevator, and that it would probably take about 10-15 minutes for that to happen, so we should just be patient.

Fifteen minutes soon turned into 30 minutes, and we were told again to just be patient, that they were working on getting us out. By now, some of the people were debating who we should call on our cell phones. One gentleman called our ship to let them know we were trapped in an elevator and to not sail without us. Someone else was trying to get through to the U.S. Embassy (as if that would do any good). For my part, I just tried to stay as composed as possible, while doing my best not to think about the fact that eleven of us were stuck in an elevator shaft, suspended by a malfunctioning cable system, some 560 feet in the air. Compounding that frightening reality was the fact that about every 15 minutes we were, once again, told to just stay calm, that help was on the way.

After a full hour passed, I could see that one particular woman, standing near me alongside her husband, was beginning to show signs of panic. That is when I decided to share with her the fact that I personally find The Serenity Prayer very consoling in times like this:

> *God grant me the serenity to accept the things I cannot change, courage to change the things I can, and wisdom to know the difference. Thy will, not mine, be done.*[46]

In the moment, I don't think that the words of the prayer were even heard by her, yet alone understood. She was scared. Then the voice on the intercom informed us that they would have to shut down the computer momentarily to see if they could reboot the system. Naturally, when they did this the air conditioner would shut off and the elevator compartment, already jammed with bodies, would get even hotter and our air space stuffier. Over the next 30 minutes, they attempted to reboot the computer again and again, each time escalating the fear level within us. At long last, after 90 minutes of being stuck between the 47th and 48th Floors, we felt the elevator moving upward. Moments later, the doors were forced open from the outside, where a half dozen men were waiting to give us a helping hand by lifting us up unto the 49th Floor Skydeck, which was about three feet higher than the floor of our elevator.

We were immediately greeted by our two bus drivers who escorted us to the elevators at the other side of the Skydeck. I was so caught up in the moment that I don't even remember observing the view outside the Skydeck windows. I just wanted to feel *terra firma* under my feet again. Once we had all descended the other elevators, we were all escorted back to the ticket booth, where our money was refunded to us, and each of us was given a small stuffed teddy bear as a memento for having gone through our ordeal. We then had to walk several blocks through town in order to rendezvous with the busses that would return us back to our cruise ship.

While waiting to cross the street, at a busy intersection, I took a moment to look up at the colossal skyscraper in which we had been suspended for an hour and a half. Just then, I was approached by the one woman whom I had perceived as being the most frightened among us during our ordeal. With a beaming smile, she reached for my hand and said, "I just want to thank you so very much for helping me through that very frightening experience. I suffer from anxiety most of the time, so you can imagine how scared I was being stuck in an elevator for 90 minutes. It was your calm demeanor, and encouraging words, that brought peace to my heart. I just wanted to thank you for your prayer. It truly saved me from having a breakdown." She squeezed my hand, said "Thank you" one more time, and then proceeded across the street with her husband.

As I slowly followed the rest of our group across the intersection,

I considered the woman's words. I turned to look, one last time, at the towering structure from which we had been delivered and thought how uneasy it must have been for eleven people to process their individual fears during those ninety minutes. I realized that I not only had the ability to bring serenity into my own inner Being, but, far more importantly, was able to share that peace with others. By God's grace, I was somehow able to comfort another person, and assuage her fear, by doing or saying something that touched her deeply within. For it is only there where true peace is to be found.

When I entered those elevator doors, my only concern was my own ascension to the Skydeck on the 49th Floor. I had no thought about the other ten people ascending alongside me. Yet, each of us had the same goal in mind. We were all hoping to reach the same destination. That consideration didn't occur to me until our mutual ascension was suspended for a period of time - time enough for me to understand.

Life is not just about our own personal ascension. We are here to help each other ascend through life, especially when we get stuck "between floors." In other words, in the same way that God is always there to help lift us up, so, too, do we share a divine duty to lift up one another – with a helping hand, a kind word, or an act of compassion. But, unless we truly understand that, our own ascension will be suspended . . . until we do.

CHAPTER 6

GOODNESS (VIRTUE)

Goodness is richer than greatness. It consists not in the
outward things we do, but in the inward thing we are.
— Edwin H. Chapin

I was always taught to look for the "good" in people. As a child, that seemed to be a fairly unnecessary exercise because, as a child, I knew of no other human quality. Aren't all people good?, I reasoned at that age. Even though I learned, later in life, that people were not always "good," I never stopped believing, for a second, that every single person is born in God's image, as pure, uncorrupted Beings. As I point out in *The Pono Principle* (2017), I make it a daily exercise to "Praise The Good In Others" at every opportunity. This principle has served me, and those who receive that praise, very well. In *12 Rules For Life* (2018), Dr. Jordan B. Peterson discusses what he terms "the essential goodness of Being:"

> *You decide to act as if existence might be justified*
> *by its goodness - if only you behaved properly. And it*
> *is that decision, that declaration of existential faith,*
> *that allows you to overcome nihilism, and resentment,*
> *and arrogance. It is that declaration of faith that*
> *keeps hatred of Being, with all its attendant evils, at*
> *bay. And, as for such faith: it is not at all the will*
> *to believe things that you know perfectly well to be*
> *false. Faith is not the childish belief in magic. That is*
> *ignorance or even willful blindness. It is instead the*
> *realization that the tragic irrationalities of life must be*

counterbalanced by an equally irrational commitment
to the essential goodness of being.[47]

Always Let Your Conscience Be Your Guide

Two years ago, would have marked my father's 100th Birthday, if he were still alive. When Dad passed away in 1999, he passed on to me a philosophy of life which has put me in good stead ever since. As I mention in the Preface of *The Pono Principle* (2017), "My father taught me *pono*. More accurately, my father demonstrated *pono* throughout his life - he lived *pono.*"[48] What that means is that he always practiced doing the right thing in all areas of his life - the very personification, and essence, of The Pono Principle.

It just so happened that I received a parcel from England on the very day that marked my father's 100th Birthday, something that I had ordered about a month earlier - Christopher Robin's Teddy Bear, "Edward." It is a beautiful replica of the Alpha Farnell teddy bear that famously inspired A. A. Milne's *Winnie the Pooh* stories. You might well wonder what a 65-year-old man was doing ordering a teddy bear for himself. I completely understand. Well, it's like this: I don't remember having a teddy bear as a child (although I very well may have had one or two). After having watched a movie about Christopher Robin, I felt motivated to buy the exact same bear that Christopher's mother bought for him for his first birthday. (Mind you, as someone who thinks that his alter ego is Peter Pan, maybe my purchase wasn't so strange after all).

Of course, the first order of business was to give my new teddy bear a name. Although his manufacturer calls him "Edward" (a tribute to the name chosen by Christopher Robin for his bear), I wanted to come up with a name that was both personal, and meaningful, to me. Since it was my father's 100th Birthday, I decided to name the bear after him - "Walter." But the more I looked at the bear, the more I thought that the name "Walter" didn't quite suit him (anymore than "Edward" did, in my opinion). But then I remembered how Dad would sometimes refer to himself as "Sir Walter" (although I know for a fact that he was never knighted by the Queen of England). And since I will forever associate my father with The Pono Principle, I decided to name my teddy bear - "Sir Walter, the Pono Bear."

Which brings me to what I believe was my new teddy bear's "purpose" for my life. Since I was a little boy, Dad always guided me by his words - and even more so by his actions - as to what doing the right thing was in all situations. He always assured me that I would know what the right thing to do was if I just followed my conscience. Despite the fact that *my conscience* was not a tangible thing that I could see with my eyes, or touch with my hands, nevertheless, I knew that it was a very real thing that I could rely on when making difficult decisions. If it helped me, as a child, to envision my conscience being an angel on my shoulder, whispering in my ear, or to imagine having Jiminy Cricket as my best friend and counselor, then so be it. As long as I believed that the right answer - to all things - was already *known* inside of me, within my own "innerness," I could grow up confident that my conscience would always guide me correctly.

And there lies the most important feature of conscience-motivated behavior - it doesn't rely on outside opinions and answers. A true act of conscience comes from deep within one's self; more specifically, from one's *True Self*. Therefore, a true act of conscience is, by definition, an act of *true self-righteousness*. A decision that comes from within our innermost conscious being is not only uniquely personal to us as individuals, but can always be relied on to be the *right* decision for us to make in any given situation. But don't expect to find any kind of *conscience* within our *False Self* for your search will be in vain.

Some time ago, I heard a fellow addict admit that she never had any kind of conscience during her years of alcoholism and drug abuse. Her *False Self* (i.e. the self-centered, unsympathetic,

uncompassionate person that the addict unconsciously morphs into)
had no ability to discern right from wrong behavior simply because
her addiction influenced every decision she made, and every action
she took. Therefore, *doing the right thing* was not part of her daily
thinking pattern. It was only when she began her 12-Step recovery
work that she discovered the presence of a *conscience* deep within
her *True Self* - that person who existed long before her addiction,
who has now risen from the wreckage of those *unconscious* years.

In our global society, people are not only expected to know
what is *ethically* right and wrong, but also what is *lawfully* right and
wrong. "Ignorance of the law is no excuse," is what we often hear
when individuals try to plead their innocence after committing a
societal crime. But, isn't it interesting that when someone commits
the most heinous of crimes - murder - there is a legal defense
available to the perpetrator if they find that person *legally* insane?
What society is basically asserting is that any *sane* individual (in
legal parlance, a "reasonable mind") would consciously *know* that
murder is the wrong thing to do (without having to take a Criminal
Law course in law school). The "insanity defense" was created
to apply in cases where a court determines that an individual,
charged with a crime, cannot discern right from wrong (i.e. has no
conscience) - therefore, by their legal definition, such an individual
must be considered insane.

I'll leave it to the brainiac attorneys, and judges, to determine
who is considered *legally* sane and insane. As a recovering alcoholic
and drug user, I can vouch for the fact that my conscience was
nowhere to be found during most of those self-absorbed years of
substance abuse and insanity. As my fellow 12-Step "Programmers"
will attest, we know all too well that our recovery depends upon
our willingness to reach a point where we "came to believe that a
Power greater than ourselves could restore us to sanity." Maybe it's
just coincidence, but that moment of clarity seems to coincide with
when my conscience "kicked back in" again.

Perhaps it is a bit silly that a man of my age would go out

and buy a teddy bear for himself, and then name the bear after his father. And maybe it's sillier still to think that "Sir Walter" would somehow be my daily reminder that I should always let my conscience be my guide. Well, I can live with silly. Silly is so much more comforting, and painless, than being insane. I truly *know* that now. In Benjamin Hoff's *The Tao of Pooh* (1982), the author puts up a strong defense for my adult *silliness*:

> *The adult is not the highest stage of development.*
> *The end of the cycle is that of the independent, clear-*
> *minded, all-seeing Child. That is the level known*
> *as wisdom. When the Tao Te Ching and other wise*
> *books say things like, 'Return to the beginning; become*
> *a child again,' that's what they're referring to. Why do*
> *the enlightened seem filled with light and happiness,*
> *like children? Why do they sometimes even look and*
> *talk like children? Because they are. The wise are*
> *Children Who Know. Their minds have been emptied*
> *of the countless minute somethings of small learning,*
> *and filled with the wisdom of the Great Nothing, the*
> *Way of the Universe.*[49]

So, Happy Belated 100th Birthday, Dad. Thank you for the many life lessons you so graciously taught me. Thank you for demonstrating unconditional love towards my mother and your two sons. Thank you for the music that filled our home either from your clarinet or your stereo console. Thank you for showing me how to navigate through the uncharted waters of life by trusting in my Creator's guiding light. And thank you for demonstrating what it is to be a man of principle, courage and, above all, humility. I suppose that I should also wish "Sir Walter" a Happy Belated Birthday, as well. It has been nice to have him around, if only to remind me of you. I send you my love and eternal gratitude - from the two of us - silly old me, and my silly old bear.

My Goodness

*You do not become good by trying to be good, but by
finding the goodness that is already within you, and
allowing that goodness to emerge.*

- Eckhart Tolle

While working through the Steps of an addiction recovery program, it is very common to beat ourselves up for the sins of our past. For many, this may be the first time we have ever had the clear-headedness - along with a newfound, sincere desire to be honest - to address the wreckage we have left in the wake of our past behavior as addicts. So when we get to a point in our recovery program where we "Made a list of all persons we had harmed, and became willing to make amends to them all,"[50] it is oftentimes suggested that we put our own names at the very top of that list.

Of course, it's completely understandable how many of the people we had harmed over the years (especially our family and closest friends) would feel far more deserving of that "Number One" spot on our amends list. After all, from their perspective, our only "claim to fame" was partying our lives away, getting in trouble with the law, losing jobs, stealing and cheating - along with a whole host of other disgusting behavior - without any regard, whatsoever, for anyone else. True as that may be for the vast majority of people gravely hurt by the behavior of alcoholics and drug abusers, it is also quite true that addicts are in no position to make those well-deserved amends to others – not until we make amends to ourselves. And the only way to do that is by putting an end to the irresponsible and self-destructive behavior we have been known for in our past.

If the common airplane emergency directive of "donning your own oxygen mask first" is helpful in illustrating this recovery program dynamic, then use it. Addicts must first be willing to completely change who they once were, behavior wise, before attempting to make amends to others they have hurt. In other words, they must go deep within themselves in order to mine for the innate goodness they were born with. One must remember what Jack Kornfield so truly states in *The Art of Forgiveness, Lovingkindness, and Peace* (2002), "Do not doubt your own basic goodness. In spite of all confusion and fear, you are born with a heart that knows what is just, loving, and beautiful."[51] That "basic goodness" does not just disappear the moment that someone becomes addicted to alcohol, drugs, or the multitude of other destructive addictions - it merely gets pushed aside and forgotten, much like a little boy's teddy bear is after the boy reaches a certain age. Rediscovering one's goodness is the only hope a recovering addict has to ever effectively make things right with those he's hurt in the past.

As stated earlier, it is very easy for those of us in recovery programs to sometimes overly focus on our bad ways, bad behavior, and bad choices demonstrated during our drinking and drugging careers. It's too easy to forget that loving, child of God we once were before we sold our souls to our addictions. I often refer to this descension as the tragic transition we make from our True God Self to our False Ego Self. It's about the loss of our True Nature, and the coming home to it in recovery.

It is my fervent belief that everyone of us possesses a spark of the Divine within us, a Divinity that we shared with God even before our birth. And it is within this divine soul that each of us "is" - the place where we find our common "God-ness" and our goodness. The mistake many of us make when we fall into the abyss of addiction is thinking that we have fallen out of God's graces. Because we believe that sin is the distance we put between ourselves and God, it's no wonder how easily we can forget that God still loves us *in spite of our sins!* Certainly, if we don't believe that God would ever forgive the grievous sins we have committed, how could we ever think that *we* could forgive ourselves?

One of the greatest blessings of an addict's "hitting bottom" is the resurrection of the mind, body and soul that often follows. Of course, I am referring to those addicts who are willing to follow a program of recovery - nay, *work* a program of recovery - which, by design, will reunite them with that higher self they used to be. And it is in that process that an addict will rediscover the goodness, and the God-ness, that has always been there, deep inside, waiting for his/her return. It is the greatest homecoming imaginable.

The power of the Parable of the Prodigal Son is in the triad of perceptions held by the father, the son, and the brother. Only the son can truly know the extent of his own sins, the weight of the tremendous guilt he bears, and the deep humiliation he fears by coming home. His dutiful brother, who has stayed in service to their father during the time of his absence, has only resentment towards him because of his sinful behavior. But, the father accepts his lost son with open arms, as though he were completely oblivious to the debauched life the son lived while he was away. It is almost as though those sins - the distance between them - never existed.

To be clear, individuals do not need to be recovering alcoholics or drug abusers to finally "come home" to their True Selves, where goodness is to be found. Many people will find that inner space of their true nature by following different spiritual paths, without having to rise from the ashes of their past destructive addictions. But the journey within, regardless of how long it takes us to embark on our individual journey, is the ultimate path of the enlightened. Like the recovering addict, Buddha would agree that the road to enlightenment begins from a place of suffering. While many look outward, towards other people and places, to find goodness in this world, the spiritual pilgrim will always discover it where he left it - in the sanctuary of his inner Being - the same place where he will find God waiting for his return home.

A "New" Normal

*I don't think we get back to normal. I think we
get to a new normal.*
- Andrew Cuomo, Governor of New York

For many years, I've walked along the Wailea beach walk in the mornings. Normally, when I do, there are numerous people also walking along the pathway, some taking scuba instruction at Ulua Beach, others practicing yoga on the expanses of open lawn, while hotel guests are either enjoying being in the swimming pools, or reading books on their chaise lounges lined up on Wailea Beach. Mothers are applying sunscreen all over their children's bodies, dads are lugging coolers down to the beach, and joggers are running by the many strolling couples who sip their coffee while conversing. As I stated, that would be an accurate description of my morning beach walk on a "normal" day. For some time now, it has looked nothing like that.

In the midst of the ongoing coronavirus pandemic, the residents here on Maui, for several months, had to deal with the same "shelter-in-place" restrictions that have been implemented throughout most of the world. With a few exceptions, they were told to pretty much stay at home. Although the beaches just recently opened to the public, for a long time only walking and jogging was allowed as long as everyone kept a distance of six feet between each other. So, for several months, it was a very strange sight to see the beaches completely devoid of human presence, with only a few people, like myself, walking along the beach walk. There are still fences along the perimeters of each of the hotel properties, and all of their outdoor lounge chairs, tables, and umbrellas have been removed. The swimming pools are still devoid of any water. Also absent are the alluring aromas of breakfast being prepared, which normally flow down from the open-air dining rooms of the different hotels as I walk by.

Assuming that the new normal of "social distancing" restrictions, along with having almost all of our hotels and small businesses still closed, continues for several more weeks - if not months - one has to wonder what life will be like when we all eventually come out of our proverbial tornado shelters to view what's left of our world out there, and attempt to reconnect with our fellow human beings. Personally, I'm far less concerned with what the state of the world will be like as I am with how we will do with this *reconnecting* thing. I suspect that whatever common fears we will have - centered around economic uncertainty, instability, and calamity - will pale in comparison to the far greater fear we will share of ever getting close to (yet alone touching) one another again.

With all of the current precautionary measures of social distancing, hand sanitizing, wearing protective masks and gloves in public, I can't help but wonder how challenging it may be for us to return to the days of giving someone a handshake, a hug, or a kiss on the cheek. Will the "new normal" be an all-out eschewal of those friendly greeting practices of old? What ultimate price will we pay, on a human level, when embracing one another no longer comes to us "naturally" anymore? What happens when we come to fear the friendly, or loving, touch of another human being? Who are we then? And what will we have lost of our humanity?

I would hope and pray that none of us would ever want to live in that type of *new* world. Since the dawn of smartphones, we have witnessed, firsthand, a steady decline in the desire to engage in direct, one-to-one communication between individuals, co-workers, and family members. The very last thing we need in *this* world, *right now,* is another reason/excuse to further disassociate with one another. Try to imagine a world where we will not only desire to forego direct verbal communication with one another (which we're already doing), but now we will also be fearful of physically getting too close to other individuals. Now, try to imagine that this world I have just illustrated is not a nightmare you will awaken from - but the "new normal" that will be this planet's future. That should scare the hell out of anyone!

Having grown up in an era when racial segregation in America was a very real thing, as was the international fear of nuclear Armageddon, I know what happens to people, and whole nations, when they feel cut off from each other, while, simultaneously, the constant threat of total annihilation hovers over their lives. Fear feeds fear. Segregation was all about fear of others (solely because they had a different skin color). And that fear was of fellow Americans! Now, compound that societal racial fear, together with a common national fear of other countries and their nuclear capabilities, and you have a world not so very different than the one we have today. The only difference is that, instead of being fearful of people of different races, now we're color-blind and fearful of everyone. Instead of worrying about the world coming to an end in a nuclear war, now we're afraid of a deadly global pandemic taking us all out. Fear is fear.

Now, just imagine that, six months from now, this whole coronavirus threat is behind us. Let's say that we still share the same global concerns, and economic uncertainty, we have today - but minus the fear. I wholeheartedly believe that we have it within ourselves to transform from a place of being fearful of having personal contact with others, to a *new* place where we use the lessons learned during this global pandemic to demonstrate a mutual respect for everyone's well-being. Maybe we find a way to convert our current predisposition to panic during crises (by hoarding toilet paper, for example), by caring for, and serving, others who have a greater need than we do. In other words, maybe we can come out of this coronavirus thing as better people.

Maybe, just maybe, this "new normal" can be reflective of a future global community coming together, as opposed to one that wishes to maintain distance from one another. Maybe we can learn from this experience that acceptance is everything when it comes to dealing with natural disasters, whether caused by extreme weather or pandemic viruses. How we choose to act, during stressful times, will often define how fearful we are as individuals. How we continue to act, after the storm has passed, more often speaks to how much compassion we have for our fellow human beings. For the sake of our shared humanity, if we do experience a "new normal" after this global pandemic, may it abound with goodness and virtue.

I, for one, will embrace **that** New World with open arms!

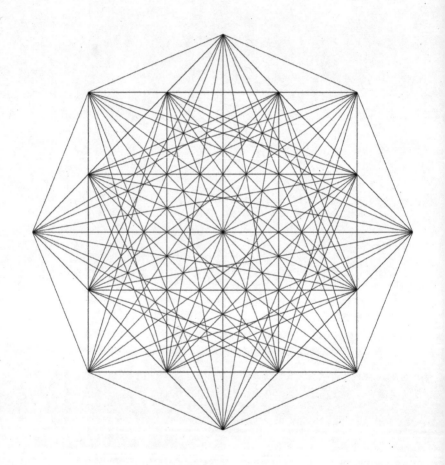

CHAPTER 7

Purpose (Aspiration)

Musicians must make music, artists must paint, poets must write if they are to be ultimately at peace with themselves. What human beings can be, they must be. They must be true to their own nature. This need we may call self-actualization.

– Abraham Maslow

I was 22 years old when I bought a one-way ticket, in steerage, aboard the S.S. *Leonardo DaVinci*, an Italian liner bound for the south of France. On March 28,1976, I sailed out of New York Harbor, bringing only one suitcase, a Martin D-35 guitar, three college semesters worth of French, and a purpose - to be a writer. With two years of military service under my belt, followed by another two years of college education, I was convinced that I had a deep enough well of experience and knowledge to draw from in order for me to begin writing short stories and, perhaps, a novel. So, off to France I sailed.

The very first person I met aboard the ship was David Bowie (whom I had just seen in concert, in Detroit, four weeks earlier). David was sailing to Naples; I was disembarking in Cannes. Although I was traveling Tourist Class, I spent the majority of my time, over the next nine days, hanging out in the First Class Lido Lounge - with David, his personal assistant, Coco, and a collective of other fascinating eccentrics who would become the inspiration for the characters in an unfinished novel I began to write decades ago. But I digress.

I only mention David because I have come to the realization, these 44 years later, that I was not the only person trying to find his purpose at the other end of that transatlantic crossing. You see, up until this auspicious voyage, David Bowie's life had been in a virtual tailspin. His cocaine addiction was well known throughout the music world, and he had just been arrested, one week earlier (in Rochester, New York), for possession of marijuana. He was now headed across the Atlantic to begin the European leg of the Thin White Duke tour. Of course, what David had no way of knowing, at that time, was that this particular crossing would take his career to new creative heights, and away from the psychosis he had experienced from excessive cocaine use. He was about to find a new purpose for his life.

Berlin was the sanctuary that saved David Bowie's career - and life. Following his European tour, he moved to an apartment on the west side of town. The Berlin Wall was symbolic of David's escape plan from the drug culture of Los Angeles, which he described as "the darkest days of my life." Berlin gave David a newfound freedom, and anonymity: "It was the first time in years that I had felt a joy of life and a great feeling of release and healing," he later said. "It's a city that's so easy to 'get lost' in – and to 'find' oneself, too."[52]

Over the next three years, David completely reinvented himself, while also transforming pop music forever. His next three albums - referred to as the Berlin Trilogy - were *Low* (1977), *"Heroes"* (1977), and *Lodger* (1979). David specifically credits the album *Low* for being "one of the better things I'd ever written. That was the start, probably for me, of a new way of looking at life." But of the Berlin Trilogy itself, he said, "It is some of the best work that the three of us have ever done. Nothing else sounded like those albums. Nothing else came close. If I never made another album, it really wouldn't matter now. My complete being is within those three. They are my DNA."[53]

It's hard for me to believe that it's been over four years since David Bowie passed away from liver cancer, at the age of 69. He was but a young 29-year-old man when I was blessed to spend those nine days sailing with him across the Atlantic. I will forever treasure my memories of him playing Jacques Brel songs (*Amsterdam* and *My Death*) on my Martin guitar, playing Tom Waits' *Shiver Me Timbers* on piano (in the Lido Lounge) while I accompanied him on guitar, and sitting on the floor in his deluxe suite, in the wee morning hours, eating scrambled eggs and lox on a huge silver platter, while drinking Chivas Regal and Rémy Martin.

The night before I disembarked in Cannes, David and Coco stayed up all night with me, and a woman with whom I had developed a close relationship. Since I was arriving on French soil the next morning, with neither a residence card nor work papers, David suggested that I stay closely tethered to this woman who had offered me a job as her chauffeur in Nice. The last photo I took of David was of him saying goodbye, while hitting a tambourine, wishing me the best as an aspiring writer. That was the last time I saw David Bowie.

Ironically, the type of writer that I "planned" on being, when I was 22 years old, never materialized over the years. Although I have a plethora of unfinished drafts of novels and short stories, some published poems and newspaper articles, and a completed screenplay to my credit, finding my true purpose as a writer didn't manifest itself until I published *The Pono Principle* in 2017. The book that I was "called" to write had absolutely nothing to do with fiction, and everything to do with truth. I am very grateful to have finally found my purpose in life, and to embrace it fully.

In the same way that David "found" his purpose in Berlin in 1976 - by recovering from addiction and exploring a new direction for his music - I also found the same pathway to recovery as David, while having discovered a more purposeful use of my writing talents. Whereas my 22-year-old Egoic Self merely wanted to impress the world with my interesting life experiences, my True Self now wishes to write about matters that are not unique to my life, but are shared by everyone, everywhere.

All of humanity is, literally, "in the same boat." Our distant ports-of-call may vary throughout our lifetimes, but ultimately we arrive at the same destination - a place where First Class and Tourist Class passengers can play music together, eat and drink together, and discuss their dreams of the future together. Only within the safe harbor of our shared humanity, our common soul, do we truly discover our purpose in life - and it is to welcome a fellow passenger aboard our mutual journey through life . . . sailing on the same ship, on the same ocean.

Bon Voyage!

Tolstoy's Journey Within

A voice seemed to cry within me, 'This is He, He
without whom there is no life. To know God and to live
are one. God is life.'
Live to seek God, and life will not be without God.
And stronger than ever rose up life within and around
me, and the light that then shone never left me again.
- Leo Tolstoy, *My Confession* (1882)

Leo Nikolayevitch Tolstoy (1828-1910) was the only writer who could get Ernest Hemingway to voluntarily relinquish his self-appointed seat at the head of the table of the greatest fiction writers of all time. In his 1950 interview with Lillian Ross in *The New Yorker*, Hemingway said:

I started out very quiet and I beat Mr. Turgenev. Then
I trained hard and I beat Mr. de Maupassant. I've
fought two draws with Mr. Stendahl, and I think I had
an edge in the last one. But nobody's going to get me in
any ring with Mr. Tolstoy unless I'm crazy or
I keep getting better.[54]

86

Perhaps the reason that Tolstoy seems to tower over all other fiction writers is simply because there are very few respectable, scholarly lists of "the greatest novels of all time" that do not place **both** *War and Peace (1869)* and *Anna Karenina (1878)* in the "top five" of whatever list you are looking at. I highlight this fact only to emphasize the monumental literary achievement of one particular novelist, Leo Tolstoy, someone who pretty much "walked away" from writing fiction (after the publication of *Anna Karenina*) so as to devote his remaining years to writing about what was going on within himself - on a philosophical, moral, and spiritual level.

Of course, such a bold, determined, decision - coming from such a literary giant as Tolstoy - sent shock waves through the international literary community. On July 27, 1883, thirty-eight days before his own death, Ivan Turgenev, another great Russian writer, wrote to Tolstoy, imploring his friend: "Turn back to literature! That is your real gift. Great poet of our Russian land, hear my plea!"[55] But Tolstoy never heeded his friend's plea. It wasn't mere vanity, or intellectual curiosity, that had Tolstoy shift his focus from literature to a personal search for God. On the contrary, Tolstoy was inexplicably drawn to a deep, inward reflection of his faith, and inner consciousness - in spite of the fact that it was against his will.

Tolstoy's was a mid-life existential crisis - and faith, not reason, ultimately saved him from his depressing thoughts (at that time) that life was meaningless, and that suicide was the only answer: "This search after a God was not an act of my reason, but a feeling, and I say this advisedly, because it was opposed to my way of thinking; it came from the heart."[56]

What I find most interesting of all, was that Tolstoy came to realize that the answers he was looking for were not to be found in his private circle of intellectual, affluent friends - but among the common peasants whose faith in God was more unshakable than the most compelling voices of "reason" that God did not exist. "The whole life of the believers of the people was a confirmation of the meaning of life which their faith gave them,"[57] Tolstoy observed of the poor, faithful masses.

What personally drew me to this pivotal, transformational point of Leo Tolstoy's life is how reflective it was of my own transition from "would-be" fiction writer to a writer of personal and spiritual growth books. Of course, the most glaring difference between our histories is the word *would-be*. Whereas Tolstoy had more than proven himself as a master of the epic novel, I merely have a footlocker filled with several unfinished manuscripts of novels, a half-dozen short stories, and one completed (and one uncompleted) screenplay. Where I can totally relate to Tolstoy's final years as a writer is in his decision to rethink the substance, and direction, of his writing. Novel writing did not fulfill him as a writer. It left him empty, and depressed.

As a *would-be* novelist, I had a very similar moment of truth when I felt a deep calling within me to write *The Pono Principle*. I suddenly came to the conclusion that fiction writing for me was strictly an ego-fulfilling goal. It was my dream to envision my books being read in university courses around the world, and to be compared to the other great novelists throughout history. The dream was all ego driven. I believe this is also what Tolstoy concluded after becoming a famous novel writer. "During that time I began to write, out of vanity, love of gain, and pride," he admitted. "How often while writing have I cudgeled my brains to conceal under the mask of indifference or pleasantry those yearnings for something better which formed the real thought of my life."

When looking back upon his writer's ego, and that of his fellow prolific writers of his day, Tolstoy says,

> We were all then convinced that it behooved us to
> speak, to write, and to print as fast as we could, as
> much as we could, and that on this depended the
> welfare of the human race. . . . Quite unconscious that

we ourselves knew nothing, that to the simplest of all
problems in life - what is right and what is
wrong - we had no answer.[58]

There you have it - even after having reached the pinnacle of literary success, his writer's ego telling him that the world's "welfare" depended on his work, Tolstoy came to the sobering conclusion that, if he didn't even have the answers to life's simplest problems - like what is right (i.e. Pono) - then his literary success was meaningless.

Since my early 20s, I had a dream of being the next Ernest Hemingway, a writer of great novels and short stories. Those who read my work, over the years - my wife, my closest friends - were very encouraging that I pursue my dream of being a writer of fiction. University professors told me that I had true writing talent. My mother's dying wish was that I write because "there is greatness there." So, when I reached a point in my life, where I felt a deeper, inner compulsion to dedicate myself to writing a personal growth book called *The Pono Principle*, imagine the shock waves that hit those closest to me, who had, for decades, encouraged me to pursue my dream of being a fiction writer. Their collective response mirrored Turgenev's plea to Tolstoy.

But, like Tolstoy, I have journeyed *within* myself as a writer, and have concluded that *The Pono Principle* may not have been the book that I would have ever expected myself to write - but I am now confident that it is certainly the book I was destined to write. This "journey within," where we reach a pivotal moment when we start asking ourselves the crucial questions of life, is the subject of this book, the one which you are reading now. Leo Tolstoy's personal search for meaning, and for God, set him on a pathway within himself - away from the external false sense of fame and fortune that brought him no comfort, no meaning, and no answers to life - to a place where he found all of the answers already waiting for him.

Tolstoy's philosophical treatise, *The Kingdom of God Is Within*

You (1894), "left an abiding impression" upon a young protester named Mohandas Gandhi (living in South Africa at the time), who listed the book as one of the three most important influences in his life. For the record, the other two books were neither *War and Peace* nor *Anna Karenina*.

A Profile In Purpose and Aspiration
- Father Richard Frechette, CP, DO

Father Richard Frechette is a Catholic priest and medical doctor who directs the Haiti programs of Nuestros Pequenos Hermanos International (NPH), and his religious community, The Passionists. These programs include orphanages, schools, a children's hospital, and mobile clinics in and around Port-au-Prince. Father Rick has carried out his double ministry over the past thirty-five years in settings of extreme poverty, violence, social upheaval, and natural disasters.

I first met Father Rick at an NPH fundraiser in Seattle some years ago. I remember telling him that evening that he was the modern-day embodiment of Father Damien of Molokai. Neither of the two priests would have ever ended up on their respective "islands of hardship," caring for the poorest of the poor, had they not volunteered to do so. I related to Father Rick how awe-inspired I have always been imagining a young 23-year-old Belgian novitiate, Damien DeVeuster, setting sail to the Hawaiian Islands (a 148-day voyage) in place of his elder brother, Pamphile, who was stricken with typhus in Louvain. Nine years later, while visiting Maui with Bishop Maigret, now Father Damien heard God's gentle whisper when he volunteered to be the parish priest of the leper colony of Kalawao, on the island of Molokai.

The turning point in Father Rick's life occurred when God's gentle whisper called to him through Mother Teresa's Sisters of Charity in Haiti. The sisters were caring for infants born of dying mothers, frequently sick with AIDS. Many of the babies did not survive, but those who did needed care, love, and a place to live. With NPH Founder, Fr. William Wasson, Fr. Rick visited Haiti and children's hospice and decided to open a new NPH home. In 1987, at the age of 34, Father Rick (along with Fr. Wasson) started NPH's first medical center in Tabarre, on the outskirts of Port-au-Prince. Appropriately, it was named St. Damien Pediatric Hospital, and it truly represents NPH's mission to serve the needs of Haiti's poorest children.

In Father Rick's autobiographical essays about his life mission as a priest and doctor, *Haiti: The God of Tough Places, the Lord of Burnt Men* (2010), he shares many extraordinary, hair-raising experiences that, oftentimes, place him in the epicenter of Haiti's underbelly, Cité Soleil. This is a dark world of violent crime, cold-blooded killers and kidnappers, and the day-to-day poverty and sickness that make mere survival the most uncertain of prospects for Haitians. Like Father Damien on his island, Father Rick represents the light of compassion which pierces through the darkness of fear that envelops his island. His light is rooted in righteousness, or what Father Damien would have known as Pono.

With regards to the triumph of Pono over fear, Father Rick says, "I can't say we were fearless. But neither were we paralyzed by fear. Our strength came from trying to do the right thing. The gospel is very clear about what the right thing is. It's never hard to figure out."[59] During one particularly trying time for the people of Haiti, there was a major revolution, and two disastrous floods. Several months later, Father Rick contracted both malaria and dengue fever. Covered in rashes, depressed and exhausted, he was relegated to lying on a mat on the floor, sweating and shivering from fever. While in this condition, Father Rick was unable to visit a dying friend, who requested to see him. Another friend was brutally killed in Port-au-Prince by gunfire. A third friend had suffered disfiguring acid burns on his face and head as a result of a witch doctor's botched exorcism. And all of this news came to Father Rick as he lay deadly sick on the floor.

Both physically and mentally, the priest had hit one of the lowest points in his life: "I wondered as I lay on the floor if there was anything about life even worth getting up for again, even if I could get up. That is a sickness. I knew it was self-pity to think that way. I knew I was nowhere near as sick as my hundreds of patients, and my life nowhere near as dire as theirs. But the cure came to me."[60] Father Rick's "cure" came in the form of community support, care and "love power." The abundance of love, compassion, and care that he had so freely given to the sick and poor of Haiti, over so many years, was returned to him tenfold - and was directly responsible for his recovery, and his determination to continue forward in his ministry of selfless medical and spiritual care.

On one particular winter solstice, a young man named Joseph, who was working at a mission hospital in Haiti, was savagely murdered in a violent section of Port-au-Prince, called "New Road." His body was left in his car to rot, then eventually taken by his killers and dumped in the scrublands, where it was eaten by animals. Since the police refused to go into the area, Father Rick was asked by Joseph's widow if he could retrieve her husband's body so that there could be a proper Christian burial. Father Rick had to negotiate with the cold-blooded killers himself, paying ransom money for Joseph's dead body, which the killers never produced (while, nonetheless, keeping the ransom paid).

During that Christmas season, Father Rick had to battle against hell itself. Following the gut-wrenching incident with Joseph, there were three other equally horrible incidents that occurred over the winter months. One can't help but to wonder what lesson, or truth, Father Rick could possibly take away from such tragedies. He writes, "In the face of the arrogant and horrible display of hell, there appears a powerful force of good capable of defying it, and often this goodness is in a seemingly very feeble form. That force of goodness has made its home in you and I."[61] There is no greater example of a "seemingly very feeble form," who enters into a direct conflict with the forces of evil, even by descending into hell to face it, than that of the crucified Christ. Yet, three days later, no greater force of goodness, no conqueror of darkness, has ever been witnessed to equal Christ resurrected. And that goodness, that light of Christ, shines within each of us.

Of course, the true heart and soul of Fr. Rick's ministry is overseeing St. Damien Pediatric Hospital. Funded through private contributions to NPH worldwide, St. Damien provides high quality medical treatment for disadvantaged and sick children in Haiti. More than half of all patients are admitted for an infectious disease such as tuberculosis, malaria, and HIV, while twenty-five percent are admitted for non-infectious diseases such as cancer, cardiovascular disease, and kidney infection. Most patients admitted are also malnourished. The outpatient clinic treats 100 children daily, for acute, parasitic, and bacterial infections. In specialized clinics, chronic conditions such as sickle cell anemia, congenital heart diseases (CHD), tuberculosis and cancer are treated for months or years if needed.

Father Rick sums up his daily challenge this way, "The poor people have scant access to medical care; even if they are lucky enough to get evaluated at a clinic, both scarcity of medicines and their relatively high prices prevent their getting treatment. Our own working conditions, especially in the poorest areas of Port-au-Prince, are tragic and are deplorable. We have little water, no electricity, few medicines and supplies."[62] But Father Rick brings more to the children of Haiti than just medical care. "We strive to bring love to them," he says. "We go where love is most needed and where it is most difficult to bring it. This is our mission."[63]

My wife, Renee, is a major sponsor of NPH; she's also a Registered Nurse. On three separate occasions, she has flown to Haiti and volunteered to assist at St. Damien Pediatric Hospital in Labor and Delivery (her specialty), and in the Pediatric Intensive Care Unit (PICU). It is there where she has worked side-by-side with the volunteer pediatric cardiologists from Gift of Life International who care for Haitian children with heart disease. And it is there where she shares the same "Christ-heart" that beats within the chests of Father Rick, the doctors and nurses, and the many other volunteer hospital workers. It is also the same "Christ-heart" that beats within every tiny chest, of every child of God, they care for at St. Damien.

As a medical doctor, Father Rick knows a lot about life and death. As a priest, he oversees the burial of about 100 destitute Haitians a week, usually carted to whatever vacant plot of State land is available at the time - in nothing more than cardboard boxes. To many, he is a living example of the Lord and Savior he worships, a touchstone of love and compassion. According to Father Rick, the word *Priest* means, "the one who offers sacrifice for the people. But the best priest is the one whose life IS a sacrifice for the people."[64]

Bless you, Father, for your selfless compassion and sacrifice.

Rick rides a motorbike through the worse slums of the city
The father and the doctor to the poorest of the poor
Raising up the future from the rubble of the past
Here, they say, 'l'espoir fait vivre,' 'hope makes life.'
- Jackson Browne, *Love Is Love*

CHAPTER 8

CONFIDENCE (CONVICTION)

I was always looking outside myself for strength and
confidence, but it comes from within.
It is there all the time.

– Anna Freud

Where do you go to find confidence? Do you call a friend, a co-worker, or your mother? Do you sit down and talk with your spouse? Your therapist? Do you stand in front of a mirror and talk to your reflection, trying to instill some confidence into the person who's doing all the talking? Better yet, why not try looking within yourself where you might discover a "better you" – someone that, maybe, the rest of the world (including yourself) has never seen before. Dr. Jordon B. Peterson addresses this in *12 Rules For Life* (2018): "You are by no means only what you already know. You are also all that which you could know, if you only would. Thus, you should never sacrifice what you could be for what you are. You should never give up the better that resides within for the security you already have - and certainly not when you have already caught a glimpse, an undeniable glimpse, of something beyond."[65]

There's No Place Like Home

Oz never did give nothing to the Tin Man
That he didn't, didn't already have.

– America, *Tin Man*

The 1939 cinematic classic, *The Wizard of Oz*, is a story about the quest of four characters who are on the road trying to find what they most desire - somewhere *out there* ("over the rainbow"). Dorothy wants to return home to Kansas, the Scarecrow wants a brain, the Tin Man wants a heart, and the Cowardly Lion wants courage. They believe that the only person in Oz who has the ability to give them what they want is the Wizard. So off they go, down the Yellow Brick Road, to Emerald City to meet the Wizard.

Of course, when they finally get to the Emerald City, the big surprise is that the Wizard is a total charlatan, and has no actual "powers" to do anything for them. What the characters learn is that each of them already had the very thing they sought. Throughout their journey, Dorothy was always wearing the magic ruby slippers that had the power to transport her and Toto back to Kansas. The Scarecrow, Tin Man, and Lion all demonstrated throughout their journey that they already possessed brains, heart, and courage, respectively.

So, why is it that these characters go to so much trouble (and danger) to seek these qualities in the external world - when they already exist *within* themselves? The obvious answer is because there wouldn't be much of a story plot unless they did. But the simple truth is, when it comes to the most important answers we seek in life, looking *within* ourselves is usually the last place we think of. From the moment we are born, we are taught that we are dependent creatures who can only find knowledge by going to schools, God by going to churches, and happiness by getting a good paying job, marrying a wonderful spouse, and living in a beautiful home with a white picket fence. We are conditioned since birth to seek all of our "creature comforts" by turning outward, instead of inward.

The problem with that type of external dependence is that it creates a false belief that it's the school that's going to make us smart, the church that's going to make us virtuous people, and a certain job, mate, or house, that's going to make us happy. The sad truth is that that is exactly what happens to most people. Believe me when I say that I am not advocating for the abolishment of all schools, churches, or the institution of marriage. I am merely saying that these external entities in our lives do not singularly, or cumulatively, hold the answers to our most important life questions.

This morning, like every morning, I did the crossword puzzle in my local daily newspaper. As you may know, the puzzles get harder throughout the week - starting with Monday - with Saturday's crossword being the most challenging. Sunday's puzzle is probably as hard as, let's say, a Thursday crossword, but only bigger. That said, there are many Friday and Saturday puzzles that scare me, when I first glance them over, because I don't *think* I know the majority of answers to the clues I'm seeing. There are even times when, after working a difficult puzzle for an hour or so, I feel like giving up.

But here lies the amazing life lesson that I have learned about my ability to do crossword puzzles, and this is the absolute truth - all the answers are already within me. Today's Saturday crossword (the week's most difficult) was no exception. At first glance, I felt that I might only know 3-4 answers off the top of my head. Yet, somehow within a two-hour timeframe, my brain was able to completely fill in the answers to every clue of that crossword puzzle. How is that possible? Did I use an *outside* source, like a dictionary? Absolutely not - I'm too much of a crossword purist to do that. (Did I mention that I only do them using an ink pen?).

My point is **not** that I am some kind of "crossword puzzle savant," or that I have a superior intellect compared to most. Certainly, as someone who has studied English in college, is a huge trivia buff, and prides himself as being a wordsmith, I'm sure that those qualities give me a huge advantage when doing something like crossword puzzles. What I am trying to emphasize here is where I end up *going* to find the answers that I need. I'm sure that, for many, the easiest resource is a dictionary, or Google search. But, over time, I have learned to *be patient* - and *trust* that the answer will eventually be found somewhere in that enormous file cabinet called my memory.

In his *Confessions*, Saint Augustine spoke at length about "the spacious palaces of memory", and how it differentiated itself from the mind alone. The deepest parts of our memory, he referred to as "wonderful storerooms," "better-concealed caverns," and "out-of-the-way inner chambers." Like me (when I do crossword puzzles), when Augustine went spelunking within these deep recesses of memory, he would say, "When I'm there, whatever it is I want, I ask for it to be produced. Certain things issue forth immediately; certain other things need a lengthy search, and it's as if they were being dug out from this or that obscure, neglected container; and certain other things charge at you in hordes: when you're asking and looking for something else, they rush into the open as if they're saying, 'Is it maybe us you want?'"[66] (10,12). So it is, too, with my own personal research projects (not just crossword puzzles) within the colossal library of my own memory bank.

Again, because of my personal history of studying English for many years, being a writer, and possessing a lot of trivial knowledge - not to mention doing crossword puzzles for most of my life - I wouldn't expect that many other people would be able to complete 100% of every crossword puzzle they attempt the way I do. But, mind you, there were 130 clues to this morning's crossword, and, at first glance, I only thought I knew 3-4 of the answers. If I didn't thoroughly *believe* that *all* 130 answers were somewhere *inside* me, tucked away in some dusty old file cabinet, I could have easily given up fifteen minutes after starting it. St. Augustine shared this same belief, and believed it to be absolutely true.

Which brings us back to the Yellow Brick Road, and our four characters searching for those desirable, virtuous qualities that, unbeknownst to them, have just been lying dormant within themselves. How very easy it would be for each of them to not *believe* they already possessed that which they were going to the Wizard to hopefully find. How easy to assume that a head full of straw couldn't possibly possess any signs of intelligence. Only after such an arduous journey as theirs, were they finally able to go deeply within themselves (where their True Selves reside) and discover, "Hey, where has this thinking brain, this loving heart, and this courage been hiding? I guess I just never thought of looking for it in here."

Just like when I saw the clue, this morning, "Artist who influenced Schiele" - initially, I drew a complete blank. But, by simply being persistent, patient, and trusting, I eventually discovered that "Klimt" was the answer to 21 Down (and I don't have to wait for the answers in Monday's newspaper to know that is correct). In other words, by believing in my True Self - the inner "me" that knows my strengths better than my False Self ever did when I was looking *out there* for answers - I have a newfound confidence that I never knew before. Going inside of myself to find the answers to life's most important questions has become my new norm. It's like coming home to the person I was meant to be.

And, as we all know, there's no place like home.

To Fly Again

The moment you doubt whether you can fly, you cease
for ever to be able to do it.
- J. M. Barrie, *Peter Pan in Kensington Gardens*

On February 9, 1953, the *Adventures of Superman* premiered on television, four days after the theatrical release of Walt Disney's *Peter Pan*. Five months later, in a maternity ward in Moline, Illinois, I also made my world debut. But it wasn't until 1958, when I was 5 years old, that I first saw the re-released *Peter Pan* in a movie theatre with my father. That was the same year when the last episode of *Superman* graced our small, black-and-white television set, in our small home in Miami, Florida. What wasn't "small" back then was the impact those two flying heroes had on the little boy I was during the 1950s. One particular Halloween, my parents bought me a Superman costume, which I gleefully put on to go trick-or-treating that evening - and then continued to wear, under my play clothes, for most of the following year or so.

My earliest dreams were of me . . . flying. No doubt, my childhood fixation on Peter Pan and Superman had everything to do with that. What I find most interesting is that these nightly dreams were episodic in nature, much like the *Adventures of Superman* that I watched on television. It wasn't like my dreams were a successive serial of one storyline, but more like individual episodes centered around my ability to fearlessly fly, and courageously "save the day." (Mind you, by this age, I was also watching *Mighty Mouse Playhouse* every Saturday morning).

What I most remember about those dreams was the sheer confidence I possessed being this heroic little boy, flying around, while helping others. How strange that after three score years I can still recall how self-assuredly I would come to the rescue of different groups of people, and just *know* that I could handle whatever dire situation they were facing. While in my dream state, I knew no fear of others, and never doubted myself. My self-confidence in my superhuman abilities was unwavering, and I knew what it felt like, internally, to be invincible.

I probably stopped having my "flying dreams" by the time I was seven or eight years old. But I have never forgotten how self-assured they made me feel, both during the dreams, and upon awakening from them. At no time during the six decades since then have I ever known that level of self-confidence, or possessed that amount of belief in myself. My early childhood dreams of flying were later replaced, years later, by reoccurring dreams about tornadoes. Simply put, I went from having dreams about this little boy who was completely fearless and invulnerable, to dreaming about a young man who was forever fearful of these ever-approaching tornadoes, while feeling completely vulnerable to their immense destructive power. What's sad is that my tornado dreams have revisited me, from time to time, ever since.

The only dream I have ever *consciously* created for myself has been my dream of being a writer. Ernest Hemingway was solely responsible for that dream. When I was 18 years old, I was stationed at a U.S. Army isolation post in West Germany. We had a small library on base, which became a personal sanctuary for me. It was there that I checked out a newly published collection of Hemingway's short stories entitled *The Nick Adams Stories*. Naturally, the central character throughout each of the stories is Nick Adams, a young boy who grows up in northern Michigan, enlists in the Red Cross ambulance corps during World War One, and then returns home, desirous of becoming a writer. This was an adventurous literary character, within a setting, that I profoundly identified with - my Michigan youth, joining the Army - and this book was the genesis of my internal desire to be a writer.

I wrote several short stories during the remaining time I served in the Army, and then returned to Michigan to attend college, with my electives gravitating towards courses in Literature and Philosophy. After three years of study, I decided it was time to buy a one-way ticket to France, where I would live the life of an American ex-patriot writer. Although Hemingway chose Paris as his writing "base of operations" in the 1920s, I was called to the French Riviera and settled in Nice. Like Hemingway, I, too, fell in with a modern-day "lost generation" of fellow ex-pats - my male friends being mostly American musicians, while English *au pairs* tended to comprise my female dating pool. I was 23 years old, in love, living in the Garden of Eden, and having the time of my life. What I wasn't doing . . . was writing.

Over the following four decades, I accumulated two foot lockers full of unfinished manuscripts of novels, short stories, stage plays and screenplays, along with hundreds of assorted cocktail napkins and pieces of scrap paper with story ideas scribbled on them. Although, during college, I did get a few of my poems published, and, many years later, completed a screenplay, what I didn't have in my writing "resume" was a published manuscript. Obviously, my dream of being a writer was to be a **published** writer - to have actual books with my name on the covers and spines, to receive residual checks from my publisher, and to do book signings in bookstores all around the world.

In the same way that I stopped having flying dreams at a certain age, I now realize that my dreams of being a writer were over the very moment I started to doubt my ability to write. The perfectionist that I was all those years created so much self-doubt within me, it's no wonder that I never completed any of my literary works. In my mind, I was afraid that my writing could never measure up to Hemingway, the source of my inspiration. How sad that we do that to ourselves. How tragic that we allow fear and self-doubt to destroy our dreams. Yet many of us do just that. But, what I have learned is that we have it within us to change our "stinking thinking" and follow through on our lifelong goals and dreams.

Three years ago, when I published my first book, *The Pono Principle*, my writing dream finally came true. All I needed to do was to go deep within myself, and rediscover that confident, self-assured little boy I once was, who could fly and help other people. Since that child and I still share the same *Being*, an identical True Nature, that "flying hero" that was me as a child still resides in my person, and so does *his* self-confidence and courage. All I have to do is beckon it again. And, once equipped with that rediscovered, and resurrected, self-confidence (which was just lying dormant for many years), I was able to complete my book, publish it, receive residual checks for it, and sign many copies of it over the past three years.

The source of all my fears, over a lifetime, have always been self-manufactured - whenever I forget who I truly am, or what I am capable of accomplishing. The best of me is not what lies on the exterior of my person, or in the rat trap of my thinking. The beauty of an oyster does not lie in its outward appearance, but what lies within its well-protected shell. Only by journeying within, to the center of my being, have I ever been able to discover the core of my True Self, where all of my strength, self-confidence, and true purpose, reside.

Only there have I found the ability to write, and to fly again.

Life As A Smorgasbord

Life is like a giant smorgasbord with more delicious
alternatives than you can ever hope to taste.

- Ray Dalio

My earliest memories of growing up in Miami, Florida, in the late 1950s and early 60s, were of going out to dinner - a lot. You see, for the most part, my mother didn't cook, and Dad's idea of fixing dinner was heating a can of pork and beans. So, we ate out a lot - not because we were wealthy, but because we were hungry. Therefore, I found myself eating in any number of all-you-can-eat buffets, cafeterias, and smorgasbord restaurants. I can vividly remember the wonderful displays of food, and the incredible variety that was available. One of my parent's favorite spots was Nohlgren's Painted Horse, on Biscayne Boulevard. The restaurant advertised their SMORG-A-STYLE way of eating this way: "Remember . . . only at Nohlgren's Painted Horse can you eat your fill of wonderful food for 99 cents. (Children Under 10, 49 cents)."

I only mention how I ate as a child, growing up in Miami, because ever since then, I have taken the same SMORG-A-STYLE approach to how I have made many of my life choices. Just like perusing the huge buffet available to me at The Painted Horse, I try to take the time to consider ALL of my options before deciding on anything. Even though I can sometimes be spontaneous in my decision-making, I really try to examine the pros and cons of, for example, where I decide to live, what I choose to eat, who I vote for, how I think - you get the idea. With rare exception, I have discovered that when I make a spontaneous decision, it is either a reflex action to something, or a momentary temptation to choose something contrary to what I consciously know is right for me.

What I often see in the world around me are many people who limit their viewpoints, and choices in life, as though they were ordering off of the original 1940 McDonald's menu - burger (with or without cheese), fries, milk shakes (3 flavors), sodas (3 flavors), coffee or milk. That's it (they think): "That's all there is in the world for me to choose from, so I'll make my choice based on that 'menu' alone." Please don't let these restaurant metaphors get in the way of what I wish to make clear - the more we can expand our minds beyond the limited choices which, at times, seem to be the only ones presented to us, the better chance we have of making, well, better choices in life.

So much of what we allow to "limit" us in life is based on our own "limited" perception, and little more. For example, if I had allowed myself to be limited to only the small "menu" of religious beliefs that were presented to me at an early age, I would never have expanded spiritually as a man (by studying other religions and spiritual beliefs). A good friend of mine once said that he was a better Catholic because of his study of, and adherence to, Buddhist teachings. I couldn't agree more. Wherever, and whenever, I find a new pathway to truth, wisdom, or light, I go. I mean, what's the alternative? To "limit" truth, wisdom, or light in my life?

Back to food choices for a second, - but only to make another observation. For me to say that I "buy into" 100% of the beliefs of any organized religion, or political party, is the equivalent of saying that I love eating every single item served on a French dinner menu (or Chinese, Greek, Cajun, or Thai, for that matter) - I simply don't. With the exception of that one guy in Ohio who has, literally, never eaten anything for dinner except meat and potatoes, I have to believe that most people probably like at least 1-2 items from a multiple of ethnic food menus. So, then how does it happen that millions (if not billions) of "individuals" strictly adhere to only one set of religious beliefs, or political ideologies - without any desire to consider alternatives - when there are so many other views to choose from? I don't get it.

My best guess is that so many of today's "individuals" are not that at all - they have lost all sense of individuality and become part of the mindless groupthink followers so prevalent in the world today. For it is mostly in organized religions, and political parties, where groupthink manifests itself so patently. And, at this particular time in history, as evidenced by the daily news, the groupthink police demand not some, but 100% of your loyalty - no perusing other ideas or "menus" for you. Independent thought, the greatest gift bestowed upon us by our Creator, has been slowly relinquished by those who find more self-worth by being "liked" on social media, but only because they "share" the same political views as their internet "friends."

But here's the problem with that. Groupthink breeds division and, oftentimes, hatred towards others - my group thinks this, your group thinks that; therefore, we are right and you are wrong. Every world conflict and, indeed, both World Wars were fought primarily for that one reason. I have a hard time believing that, if every religion known to man, and every political leader throughout history, demonstrated a sincere interest in the alternative views of others, we would never have experienced such a history of religious and political strife.

Inclusiveness of other "foreign" points of view enrich our collective lives in the same way that sampling a taste from the wide variety of foods served at a buffet enriches our appreciation of international cuisines. As one who has held onto a central religious belief for most of my life, and stayed true to certain political principles, I still maintain an openness to hearing how other spiritual and political ideas can better me as a man, and the world we share together. I've never really been a meat and potatoes kind of guy. Show me the way to the buffet table.

And let's all eat together.

CHAPTER 9

LOVE (COMPASSION)

*Find the love you seek, by first finding the love within
yourself. Learn to rest in that place within
you that is your true home.*

— Sri Sri Ravi Shankar

As I stated in the first chapter: we are stardust. As cosmic creations, bonded by our universal DNA, we share much more than just our genetic composition. We have human needs, unique to our species. Perhaps the most important of our shared human needs is our desire to be loved. Ilia Delio, a Franciscan sister and scientist, puts it this way in *The Unbearable Wholeness of Being* (2013):

> *Every human person desires to love and to be loved, to*
> *belong to another, because we come from another. We*
> *are born social and relational. We yearn to belong, to*
> *be part of a larger whole that includes not only friends*
> *and family but neighbors, community, trees, flowers,*
> *sun, earth, stars. We are born of nature and are part of*
> *nature; that is, we are born into a web of life and are*
> *part of a web of life. We cannot know what this means,*
> *however, without seeing ourselves within the story of*
> *the Big Bang universe. Human life must be traced back*
> *to the time when life was deeply one, a Singularity,*
> *whereby the intensity of mass-energy exploded into*
> *consciousness. Deep in our DNA we belong to the*
> *stars, the trees, and the galaxies. . . . Deep within*
> *we long for unity because, at the most fundamental*

> *level, we are already one. We belong to one another*
> *because we have the same source of love; the love that*
> *flows through the trees is the same love that flows*
> *through my being; the love that etches the trace of*
> *transcendence on my neighbor's face is the same love*
> *that details my own face. We are deeply connected in*
> *this flow of love, beginning on the level of nature where*
> *we are the closest of kin because the*
> *earth is our mother.*[67]

As you move into the world, find ways of extending lovingkindness to yourself and others in practical ways. Remember that love is the very foundation of the universe. You are simply a conduit for the inflow and outflow of love.

I Am Love

> *And now these three remain: faith, hope, and love. But*
> *the greatest of these is love.*
> - 1 Corinthians 13:13 (NIV)

For something that represents what I believe to be the core of all existence - our universe, our very essence, one's primary gift to the world - the word *Love* is so very often misused, misidentified, misconstrued, and/or misdirected. How is it that we can say that we "love" someone while, simultaneously, declaring that we are not "in love" with that same person? Where exactly does that line of demarcation exist between only *liking* something and *loving* something? Do I really "love" the Beatles, garlic fries, and tropical sunsets - or am I grossly exaggerating the proper use of the word?

Why do we use the term "love" to describe how we respond to those Beatles songs, or that basket of hot garlic fries at a ballgame, simply because we're *receiving* some type of deep satisfaction that makes us somewhat euphoric in the moment? And, if we are so liberal with the word *love* to describe those types of things, then how "meaningful" is it when we use the same word to describe how much we *love* our children? Or how much we *love* God?

It's my view that, when used as a verb, *love* tends to lose much of the magnitude of meaning that it enjoys as a noun. Returning to the Beatles for a moment, I believe that there is much more profundity in the proclamation "All You Need Is Love" than there is in "She Loves You (Yeah, Yeah, Yeah)." Yeah, this girl might love you right now, but what happens over time, when she finds out you snore at night, or that you are still pining over an ex-girlfriend, let's say? Her (*verb*-al) love for you will probably go the way of the wind. But, you sir, will still possess the basic human need to deeply feel love, whether it comes from her, someone else, or your own self.

And, there lies the rub. If we, as human beings, go through life without fully understanding that true love resides *within* us, then we will forever be dependent upon others to supply us with this most common, and vital, human need. In other words, how are we ever going to practice the verbs of *truly* loving another, or *truly* being in love with another, if we don't first discover the (noun) love within our True Selves - the only place where *true* love exists?

Am I suggesting that much of what we think of as love is meaningless if it originates from our egoic False Self? That's an affirmative. By definition, a *false* self cannot possibly understand what *true* love is. Since the ego is primarily obsessed with self-love, it is impossible to ever give the gift of love to another in the way that he or she deserves to be loved. Such is the ultimate curse of selfish, self-centered individuals - they are simply incapable of true love, which is always a self-*less* act.

It's a horrible thing when you realize that you have spent the majority of your life unable to truly love others. Usually, it's because your primary focus has, for the most part, always been on your Ego Self, that character you seem to like to portray to the rest of the world, and to yourself. Unfortunately, there are those who spend an entire lifetime portraying such a tragic character, and consequently go to their graves never knowing true love. From Sophocles to Shakespeare, we have seen multiple examples of characters with tragic flaws (hamartias), oftentimes stemming from prideful egos. Who among us would actually want to emulate such tragic characters? Truth is, many of us do.

Certainly, people who are self-obsessed would find it very difficult to put others before themselves - there lies their tragic flaw. No matter how much they try to love others, even their own family members, their love of self will always trump their vain (meant both ways) attempts. As long as these "actors" insist on only portraying this false image of themselves, the rest of the world will never receive from them anything that is real or truly meaningful - they will only continue to witness a tragic actor's performance on life's stage. But what happens when an actor addresses his or her tragic flaws, and decidedly takes steps to overcome them?

Redemption, Resurrection, Recovery - these are the gateways to the True Self that has been hidden deep within the prideful actor all along. Whatever event has brought the actor to his knees will be the saving grace responsible for guiding this now humble individual to the light of his True Self, where true love resides. A newfound gratitude will flow from within his soul, and grow in proportion to the degree in which the True Self is more deeply mined and nurtured. As the individual continues to take a sledgehammer to destroy the old False Self - that selfish, egocentric, self-created actor they once were - only then will they discover that they not only possess true love within themselves . . . they *are* that true love!

Once we become aware that love is part of our very essence, we return to that pure, loving newborn we were when we first entered this world, spotless and uncorrupted. We re-awaken to the simple truth that we were born to *be* Love. Our gift to the world is to *be* the Love that our world needs to survive and flourish. In the same way that God sent His Son, Jesus, to be that gift to all humankind, so too are we sent with the same mission. Jesus was the ultimate example of Love for us to follow. When asked to sum up God's mission for us, He replied, "Love the Lord your God with all your heart and with all your soul and . . . Love your neighbor as yourself"[68] (Mark 12:30-31). In other words, Jesus's primary testament to humankind was simply this: "All you need is Love."

And He said it 2,000 years before the Beatles did.

We Are One

We are one, after all, you and I, together we suffer,
together exist and forever will recreate one another.
- Pierre Teilhard de Chardin

On March 15, 2019, during Friday Prayer at two separate mosques in Christchurch, New Zealand, an armed individual indiscriminately murdered 50 innocent people, between the ages of 3 and 77 years old. The first victim was a Muslim man who greeted the individual at the entrance to the Al Noor Mosque with the words, "Hello, Brother." For the next six minutes, a total of 42 worshipping Muslims were either gunned down near the entrance to the mosque, or in the small prayer room, where the majority of the carnage occurred. The killer briefly returned to his vehicle, to retrieve another weapon, only to go back to the prayer room and mercilessly shoot many of the already wounded victims. Exiting the Al Noor Mosque, the killer murdered a woman outside, as she begged for help, and then left the scene in his vehicle, to the music of "Fire" by The Crazy World of Arthur Brown, where the singer screams: "I am the god of hellfire!"

The killer then drove about three miles to the second mosque at the Linwood Islamic Centre. There, he began to shoot worshippers, both outside and inside the small wooden structure. One worshipper grabbed a credit card reader, ran out of the mosque, and threw the reader at the coward. He then attempted to draw the attention of the killer, but the murderer entered the mosque and continued firing. When the killer returned to his car again, the Muslim threw a discarded shotgun at his car, shattering its windshield. The coward then drove away. Within minutes, local police rammed his car, and arrested him at gunpoint.

In a city named in honor of Jesus, the "Prince of Peace," in a country famous for being a safe haven for all, pure evil was unleashed on innocent human beings as they prayed together in their religious sanctuary. Whatever prayers were being said in that moment, whatever loving words were coming from the lips of those inside the mosques, were suddenly interrupted by the sharp, unearthly sound of gunfire and human screaming. The evil rampage that occurred at the two Christchurch mosques lasted less than 15 minutes, but the ripple of what happened there, during those tragic minutes, immediately spread throughout the local community, New Zealand, and the rest of the world. One ripple reached the island of Maui - 5,000 miles across the Pacific Ocean.

The Lei of Aloha for World Peace was the brainchild of a very good friend of mine, Ron Panzo. After the terror attacks in Paris, in November 2015, Ron was moved by compassion and sympathy for the people of Paris and decided that they "needed a hug." The action step he took manifested itself in a mile-long Lei of Aloha made of intertwined stands of ti leaves, 20 feet long, that are then intertwined together into a rope of 33 strands. Eight of those 20-foot ropes equals one-mile of lei. (I discuss the Lei of Aloha, in much further detail, in my book *The Pono Principle*).

Delegates of Lei of Aloha for World Peace delivered that first lei to Paris - and subsequently, following each of the terrorist attacks in Orlando, Parkland, and Las Vegas. When the news came about the mosque killings in Christchurch, a delegation was immediately formed to travel to New Zealand with a lei. Over the weekend, there were over 300 volunteers (mostly local, but some vacationing visitors) who helped weave 14 truckloads of ti leaves into the mile-long Lei of Aloha. I traveled with the delegation of four other representatives from Maui to deliver the lei to the people of Christchurch, the two mosques, the first responders, and the hospital that cared for the shooting victims.

Along with the other four delegates, I was given a Lei of Aloha t-shirt to wear during our presentation ceremonies. Written on the back of the shirt are the words "WE ARE ONE," followed by the organization's mission statement. During the four days we were there, many people approached us about the t-shirts, because they read what was written on the back, and assumed that they were created to pay respect to the victims of the Christchurch mass shootings. Also, the term "We Are One" was used on many occasions, over the weekend, during speeches given by New Zealand Prime Minister Jacinda Ardern, Christchurch Mayor Lianne Dalziel, the Imams from the mosques, and on many of the posters and cards that were left at the memorial areas near the two mosques and the Christchurch Botanic Gardens. The very message we were bringing from Hawaii was the same message being echoed in New Zealand - We Are One.

The first lei was presented, across the street from the Al Noor Mosque, into the hands of representatives of the Muslim community, Christchurch mayor Lianne Dalziel, representatives from Ngāi Tahu (Māori people from the southern island of New Zealand), and emergency services. After draping the first lei over the front fence of the Al Noor Mosque, we then presented three leis to the New Zealand Police, St. John Ambulance, and Victim Support. After that, we presented leis at the Linwood Mosque, Christchurch Botanic Gardens, and Christchurch Hospital.

It was at the Linwood Mosque that I felt the strongest spiritual connection to the people most affected by this tragic, senseless act of violence - the Muslim community. As eight of us stood along the fence, just outside the entrance to the mosque, holding the 20-foot lei, we waited for those inside to finish their prayers. I'll never forget the faces of the worshippers as they slowly began to look outside to see us standing there, all in a row, holding this lei as an offering to them. Eight innocent people where indiscriminately murdered at that very spot only ten days earlier. And here were eight strangers to their mosque, bringing them a symbol of unity - that had the loving spirit (mana) of over 300 people intertwined within its leaves - and had traveled 5,000 miles to be presented to them.

As the dozen or so worshippers slowly exited the mosque, they lined up along the mosque wall, facing us. One young Muslim woman, standing directly in front of me, was passionately sobbing. Wearing a dark green hijab, her face wore the pain of her faith community. As we slowly walked forward, presenting the lei to the line of Muslims facing us, I felt as though we were bridging any imagined gap that exists between our cultures, our countries, or our religious faiths. We did not hand off the lei to them, but stood together, eye-to-eye with our Muslim brothers and sisters, all of our hands holding this symbol of oneness and aloha. My hands were interspaced between those of the Muslim man (who had attacked the cowardly killer with the credit card reader, smashed his windshield, and chased after his car as he sped off) and the hands of the sobbing young Muslim woman.

The wind was blowing, and a small white flower from the tree above us landed on my wrist. Even as the wind continued to blow, over the time we stood there - together as one, holding the lei - the flower never blew off my wrist. At this point, the Imam went into the mosque, returning with a box, from which he handed out copies of the Quran to be given to us as gifts. A young Muslim man presented me with my copy saying, "It is the most precious thing we have to give you." His words touched my inner soul and, in that moment in time, he and I were truly one in spirit.

Before I left for Christchurch, my friend Ron perfectly summed up the mission of Lei of Aloha for World Peace, answering why people from the most remote island chain in the world would travel so far to bring healing compassion to those who needed it most:

"Some say it's the ocean that separates us, but those of us in Polynesia know that it is, in fact, the ocean that connects us."

As I received the precious gift of the Quran from the young Muslim man presenting it to me, I saw that the small white flower that had alighted on my wrist, was still there, and so I carefully placed it inside the Quran to act as a bookmark forevermore. That flower, which had bloomed from a tree at the Linwood Mosque, is an eternal reminder that we are, indeed, one.

For the Love of God

What is the difference between the power of God and the power of man? In one of his most enlightening meditations, Presbyterian minister Frederick Buechner addresses this question most succinctly and accurately. In *The Magnificent Defeat* (1966), he makes the case, as sad as it is to admit, that "man's most absolute power, the one that he can be surest of because it involves nothing except power, is his power to destroy."[69] Any general overview of world history will display the bloody thread of war between tribes, nations, religions, and political ideologies. Ever since 1945, the birth of the Atomic Age, man now has the ability to destroy all life on this planet. That, Buechner argues, is man's most "absolute" power.

But man also has the ability to create. Look around you. Go to an art museum. Observe a jet airplane soar through the sky. Call your best friend, in France, on your Apple Watch. Join a religious group, or a political party. These are all products of man's creative powers. The one thing they all share in common, according to Buechner, is that they are all "external and coercive." Man's power ends at the entrance to the internal. A medical doctor might be able to perform open-heart surgery, but only the Great Physician, Jesus Christ, has the ability to administer to the human soul. And what is the deepest longing within the human soul? It is to know love, peace, purpose, and God – things that are beyond the scope of man's power. Mostly, we want to know the love of God, deeply within our inner Beings. Buechner puts it this way:

> So the power of God stands in violent contrast with the
> power of man. It is not external like man's power, but
> internal. By applying external pressure, I can make a
> person do what I want him to do. This is man's power.
> But as for making him be what I want him to be,
> without at the same time destroying his freedom, only
> love can make this happen. And love makes it happen
> not coercively, but by creating a situation in which, of
> our own free will, we want to be what love wants us to
> be. And because God's love is uncoercive and treasures
> are freedom - if above all he wants us to love him, then
> we must be left free not to love him - we are free to
> resist it, deny it, crucify it finally, which we do again
> and again. This is our terrible freedom, which love
> refuses to overpower so that, in this, the greatest of all
> powers, God's power, is itself powerless.[70]

It is absolutely true that we possess the free will not to love God. It is also within the purview of our sacred free will not to love others. To be frank, there are self-loathing individuals who don't even have the capacity to love themselves. How abysmally tragic is it that the greatest gift we have to give to the world, and to receive from others, is, at the end of the day, purely a matter of choice, left to the whims of our personal free will? But where does this free will "love valve" exist, this regulator of emotional affection that we can either open or close at any time? Is there an on/off switch on our chests, outside of where our hearts are located? No, there is no external valve or switch to regulate love. Certainly, love may be displayed, externally - with embraces, kisses, red roses, and boxes of Godiva chocolates - but let us never forget that True Love is generated from *within* us. Perhaps, more importantly, is the fact that the place we receive love is also within the deepest recesses of our inner Being. And the internal barometer we use to measure one's love is its depth (*How Deep Is Your Love* asked the Bee Gees).

Although I wrote about this in *The Pono Principle* (2017), what I am about to say bears repeating. It may be the most important truth I know and, therefore, the most important truth I have to impart to you, the reader. As human beings, we certainly possess the gift of free will, the ability to make free choices in life. We also have the ability to choose whether or not to believe in God (or a Higher Power). But, regardless of whether or not we adhere to any one religion or spiritual philosophy, we still possess the free will to incorporate the most beneficial truths we learn from different religions into our own lives. My point is that you don't have to be a Christian to understand the power in the words of this young son of a Jewish carpenter:

> *Love the Lord your God with all your heart and with all your soul and with all your mind. This is the first and greatest commandment. And the second is like it: Love your neighbor as yourself. All the Law and the Prophets hang on these two commandments.*[71]
>
> - Matthew 22:36-40

And what is it that we are told to love with? Our hearts, our souls, and our minds – the very components of our inner Beings. No sacrificial lambs, no burnt offerings, no roses, and no Belgian chocolates; in other words, nothing that is external. We are simply asked to love – nay, we are *commanded* to love - with everything our Creator placed inside of us, the totality of our Being, our True Self. Only when we ascend to that sacred universe within ourselves will we find that storehouse of Love just waiting for us to share with our fellow brothers and sisters.

Love is our greatest gift - to ourselves, to others, and to God. Be generous with it. Dish out large portions of it, and when people request a second serving, gladly give it to them. I can think of no surer way to a brighter tomorrow, for absolutely every living creature, than by our daily commitment to spread love where we

119

Robert DeVinck

can. We not only have the ability, but also the moral responsibility, to leave our children and grandchildren a better world. It is the Light of Love, which glows within each of us, that is truly the greatest gift we can bestow upon our world today . . . the one we will leave to their care tomorrow.

AFTERWORD

Today marks the tenth anniversary of my "internal" homecoming. That was the first day of my sobriety, the day when I began to rediscover my True Self, the person my Divine Father created me to be. Clear-headed and penitent for the first time in 41 years, the prodigal son that I was had no earthly father or mother to embrace upon my return to the land of the living - for they no longer resided there. I had waited too long to come back home. By this time, all of my children had grown and moved out of our family home, and my wife and I had agreed to physically separate. In recovery parlance, I had hit my bottom, or, at least, I could clearly see it just below me - amid the scrapheap and wreckage caused by my past addictive behavior.

What I soon discovered was, when one's starting point is the bottom, then ascension is the only possible road forward. I followed that road straight into a 12-Step Recovery Program, where I was embraced by a non-judgmental, empathetic Fellowship of other prodigal sons and daughters who had also come home to the solace of those meeting rooms. There, I was guided through the recovery Steps, all of wish led me to the common workshop where all addicts must journey to face their demons and reconnect to their higher selves - that sacred place within ourselves, which we had all but forgotten was always there, just waiting for our return.

Over these past ten years of recovery work - within myself - I have rediscovered all of the most important things that I lost during my 41-year drinking career: God, Truth, Consciousness, Happiness, Peace, Goodness, Purpose, Confidence and Love. These were the gifts given to me at birth, gifts that I treasured as a child, but recklessly squandered away over a lifetime of selfish and self-centered thoughts and actions. Had I never taken that first step, had

I never ascended within, to reconnect with my True Self, I would never have been able to find, again, those gifted treasures bestowed upon me at birth.

I promise you, this same treasure trove exists within each of us, ever-present and anxious to be found. While most individuals waste years – in some cases, whole lifetimes - searching "out there" for these essentials of life, what is tragic is that the last place they ever think of looking for these things is *within* themselves. And, like King Tutankhamen's tomb, hidden for over 3,000 years, it would never have been discovered if not for an individual's determined quest to find it. This is the necessary ingredient to discovering the treasures of our inner selves – a firm determination to dig deep within the soil of our souls.

The personal reward for taking the journey within, along with the hard work of steady excavation, pays off in Divine Dividends. As I mentioned, my parents both passed away prior to my sobriety date (ten years ago today). But I now have seven grandchildren, all of whom were born since I became sober. Over their lifetimes, they may hear snippets of stories, from their parents or grandmother, that they may find hard to believe. Stories about a man who put himself before his family, who let his addictions kidnap the best of himself. I can't control what they *hear* about their grandfather's behavior prior to their births. What I can control is what they *see* in their grandfather during the time they have to share with him during his remaining years. Simply stated, not one of them will ever have to *know* the man I was before I became the man I am today, the man I was created to be. This is the greatest Divine Dividend of all, one that I am so very grateful to God for on this very special day – this day that marks my 10 years of sobriety - this day when I am writing these closing words to this book - and, on top of it all, it's Father's Day. Thank you, dear God, my Divine Father, for this day!

As I embark on my personal quest towards acquiring a doctoral degree in Psychology, I can clearly see how my inner development is a classic example of what Carl Jung referred to as Individuation – becoming what you already are potentially, but now more deeply and more consciously. This newfound, rediscovered conscious awareness has delivered me to a state of wholeness, which is the goal of the individuation process of transformation and renewal. As Ken Wilber says in *Up from Eden* (1996), "The rediscovery of this infinite and eternal Wholeness is man's single greatest need and want."[72]

This book you are reading is about my coming home - after having spent over two-thirds of my life searching the world over to find the answers to life's two most important questions: "Who am I?" and "Where is God?" Only when I returned home, to rediscover my True Self, were both questions answered simultaneously. In *The Unbearable Wholeness of Being* (2013), Ilia Delio sums up my experience perfectly:

> *Authenticity of self reveals God; in being oneself one*
> *expresses God. When divine love becomes incarnate in*
> *us, Christ is born anew. . . .*
> *We are held by an embrace of Love, a 'love-field'*
> *sustaining us at every moment. This field of love is*
> *God, the hidden depth and core of being that makes*
> *wholeness of being possible. We must discover this*
> *love for the evolution of human life and this means*
> *coming home to ourselves and being home within*
> *ourselves. This coming home to ourselves is being at*
> *home in God.*[73]

This prodigal son has finally returned home, to find himself enwrapped within the welcoming embrace of his Divine Father. Through His great mercy, and unconditional love, He has received me with open arms. My lifelong journey has brought me home again, where the Light of Love now burns brightly within the deepest recesses of my inner Being. This is the fire which warms my soul, which is stoked by the love I have for my Creator, a love I wish to share with those whose lives have touched mine.

May your personal journey deliver you home again - to the warm embrace of a loving God, the One who was content to wait for your return, to the place where He has always resided – within His Divine Creation . . . You.

A FINAL EXHORTATION

Ascend, brothers, ascend eagerly, and be resolved in your hearts to ascend and hear Him who says: Come and let us go up to the mountain of the Lord and to the house of our God, who makes our feet like hind's feet, and sets us on high places, that we may be victorious with his song. Run, I beseech you, with him who said: Let us hasten until we attain to the unity of faith and of the knowledge of God, to mature manhood, to the measure of the stature of the fulness of Christ, who, when He was baptized in the thirtieth year of His visible age, attained the thirtieth step in the spiritual ladder; since God is indeed love, to whom be praise, dominion, power, in whom is and was and will be the cause of all goodness throughout infinite ages.
Amen.[74]

- Saint John Climacus,
The Ladder of Divine Ascent (ca. 600 AD)

ACKNOWLEDGEMENTS

On this particular journey towards publication, I feel most indebted to those who have taken the spiritual journey within, long before I did, and shared that experience to the world. From St. Augustine to Fr. Richard Rohr, from Siddhartha Gautama to Sri Swami Satchidananda, from Socrates to Carl Jung - from the greatest minds known to humankind - I learned that, at some transformative moment in our lives, we eventually have to turn inward in order to find the answers to life that our outward search was never able to uncover. To these great saints and sages of history, I owe everything. They were the ones who guided me to the entrance of the inner cave of my being, handed me a torch, and encouraged me to go as deeply as possible. There, and only there, they promised, would I find the hidden treasure of my soul.

I am so very grateful to the writers, far too many to name, who spoke to my inner Being from the time I first devoured their words, as a young boy, not even ten years old, at the Babcock Park Library in Hialeah, Florida. Even today, at this very moment, I have the miraculous ability to immediately transport myself through time and space, to my Army barracks in West Germany in 1972, lying on my bunk, reading a Hemingway short story for the first time, a tale that had the miraculous ability to immediately transport me to a campfire setting, alongside a railroad embankment, in northern Michigan. There, within the story, I had the miraculous ability to actually *see* Nick, Bugs, and Ad sharing ham, eggs, and bread around a fire beneath a canopy of beechwood trees; I could also *smell* the ham frying, *hear* the sizzling grease sputter in the skillet, and even *taste* the hot ham fat sopped up with a slice of bread. This is how literature exists in our lives - not by sitting dormant on public library bookshelves, but by being sopped up internally, forever, within the library of our memories.

So, too, is it with music. I wish to thank all of the great composers, and singer/songwriters, whose artistic compositions still play within the music library of my memory, music that also has the miraculous ability to transport me through time and space, to very special moments in my life – where the music is forever attached to a certain person, or a specific place or time. But, as amazing as it is that an individual can remember the lyrics to hundreds (if not thousands) of songs, and can also associate special memories to each of those songs, in truth, that is merely a testament to what *we* have the ability to do within the deep caverns of our memory. I'm far more in awe of, and grateful for, the profound and extremely personal mining that an artist has to do, within their own inner caverns, in order to create a timeless piece of music. To my two favorite singer/songwriters, Joni Mitchell and Jacques Brel, I thank you for sharing your innermost selves with the rest of humanity, and for touching my innermost self in the process.

What I am most grateful for is the grace of wisdom to now see how all of our internal thoughts, our deepest truths, and our most precious memories – when shared – have the miraculous ability to transform other people, all of whom share a common cosmic DNA - by becoming part of their internal thoughts, memories, and truths. It is in this way that we can clearly see how truly connected we are to each other, and to the universe around us. The ultimate truth – what I call the win/win/win philosophy of The Pono Principle – is manifested when our greatest reward, our ascension within ourselves, becomes our greatest gift to others, and to the entire world.

Mahalo, ke Akua!

ENDNOTES

Chapter 1

1   Delio, Ilia. "Love at the Heart of the Universe," "The Perennial Tradition," *Oneing*, vol. 1, no. 1 (Center for Action and Contemplation: 2013), 21-22.

2   *The Holy Bible: New International Version.* (Grand Rapids: Zondervan, 2011).

3   Ibid.

4   Ibid.

5   *The Bible.* Authorized King James Version, (Oxford UP, 1998).

6   Nouwen, Henri J. M. *The Return of the Prodigal Son.* (New York: Convergent, 2016), 20.

7   Ibid, 20-21.

8   Satchidananda, Swami. *Truth is One; Paths are Many.* [Blog post]. Retrieved from http//www.lotusindia.org, 2019.

9   Haigh, Martin. "The Crucifix on Everest," *Reader's Digest*, August 2008, UK edition, 44.

10 Ibid, 46.

11 Ibid, 46.

12 Ibid, 46.

13 Hillary, Edmond. *High Adventure.* (New York: Oxford, 1955), 229.

14 Haigh, Martin. "The Crucifix on Everest," *Reader's Digest*, August 2008, UK edition, 48.

15 Bonaventure. *The Soul's Journey Into God.* (Mahwah: Paulist Press, 1978), 21

16 *The Holy Bible: New International Version.* (Grand Rapids: Zondervan, 2011).

17 Huxley, Aldous. *The Perennial Philosophy.* (New York: Harper Perennial, 2009), vii.

18 Rohr, Richard. *Immortal Diamond.* (San Francisco: Jossey-Bass, 2013), xii-xiv.

19 Peterson, Jordan B. *12 Rules For Life: An Antidote to Chaos.* (Toronto: Random House Canada, 2018), 60.

20 Rohr, Richard. *Divine DNA.* [Blog post]. Retrieved from http//www.cac.org, 2017.

Chapter 2

21 Voltaire. *The Works of Voltaire: A Philosophical Dictionary, Vol. XIV.* (Paris: E. R. DuMont, 1901), 130.

22 *The Holy Bible: New International Version.* (Grand Rapids: Zondervan, 2011).

23 Voltaire. *The Works of Voltaire: A Philosophical Dictionary, Vol. IX.* (Paris: E. R. DuMont, 1901), 215.

24 Voltaire. *The Works of Voltaire: A Philosophical Dictionary, Vol. I.* (Paris: E. R. DuMont, 1901), 52.

25 Ibid, 30.

26 Ibid, 31.

Chapter 3

27 27 Ray, Reginald A. *The Awakening Body.* (Boulder: Shambhala, 2016), 67.

28 Glickman, Marshall. *Beyond the Breath.* (North Clarendon: Journey Editions, 2002), 115.

29 Peterson, Jordan B. *12 Rules For Life: An Antidote to Chaos.* (Toronto: Random House Canada, 2018), 362.

30 *The Holy Bible: New International Version.* (Grand Rapids: Zondervan, 2011).

31 *The Holy Bible: Douay-Rheims Version.* (London: Baronius Press, 2006).

32 Rohr, Richard. *Immortal Diamond.* (San Francisco: Jossey-Bass, 2013), xii.

33 Wilber, Ken. *The Simple Feeling of Being.* (Boston: Shambhala, 2004), 4.

34 Wilber, Ken. *The Collected Works of Ken Wilber, vol. 8: One Taste.* (Boston: Shambala, 2000), 448-449.

Chapter 4

35 Bach, Richard. *Illusions.* (London: Arrow Books, 1977), 41.

36 Buechner, Frederick. *The Magnificent Defeat.* (New York: Harper One, 1966), 132.

37 Ibid, 135.

38 Augustine. *Confessions.* (New York: Modern Library, 2017), 304.

39 Ibid, 306.

40 Ibid, 307.

41 Ibid, 308.

42 Yogananda, Paramahansa. *Autobiography of a Yogi.* (Los Angeles: Self-Realization Fellowship, 2015), 173.

Chapter 5

43 Satchidananda, Swami. *How to Have a Peaceful Life.* [Blog post]. Retrieved from http//www.swamisatchidananda.org, 2019.

44 Satchidananda, Swami. "You Observe the Day and You Receive the Benefit – July 9" (note). *Facebook.* 8 July 2014, 2:57 PM. www.facebook.com/sriswamisatchidananda. Accessed 14 June 2020.

45 Peterson, Jordan B. *12 Rules For Life: An Antidote to Chaos.* (Toronto: Random House Canada, 2018), 357.

46 Alcoholics Anonymous. *Twelve Steps and Twelve Traditions.* (New York: A.A. World Services, 2009), 41.

Chapter 6

47 Peterson, Jordan B. *12 Rules For Life: An Antidote to Chaos.* (Toronto: Random House Canada, 2018), 107.

48 DeVinck, Robert. *The Pono Principle: Doing the Right Thing in All Things.* (Bloomington: Balboa Press, 2017), xi.

49 Hoff, Benjamin. *The Tao of Pooh.* (New York: Dutton, 1982), 151.

50 Alcoholics Anonymous. *Alcoholics Anonymous, 4th Edition.* (New York: A.A. World Services, 2001), 59.

51 Kornfield, Jack. *The Art of Forgiveness, Lovingkindness, and Peace.* (New York: Bantam Books, 2002), 9.

Chapter 7

52 Hughes, Rob. *David Bowie remembers Berlin: 'I can't express the feeling of freedom I felt there.'* [Blog post]. Retrieved from http//www.uncut.co.uk, 6 Jan 2017.

53 Pegg, Nicholas. *The Complete David Bowie.* (London: Titan Books, 2016), 389.
54 Ross, Lillian. "How Do You Like it Now, Gentlemen?," *The New Yorker,* 6 May 1950.
55 Zweig, Stefan. *The Living Thoughts of Tolstoi.* (New York: Longmans, Green & Co., 1939), 1.
56 Ibid, 50.
57 Ibid, 45.
58 Ibid, 31.
59 Frechette, Richard. *Haiti: The God of Tough Places, the Lord of Burnt Men.* (New Brunswick: Transaction Publishers, 2010), 6.
60 Ibid, 32.
61 Ibid, 39.
62 Nuestros Pequeños Hermanos (NPH). *About Us: Leaders: Fr. Rick Frechette C.P., DO.* http//www.nph.org, 2020.
63 Frechette, Richard. *Haiti: The God of Tough Places, the Lord of Burnt Men.* (New Brunswick: Transaction Publishers, 2010), 44.
64 Ibid, 73.

Chapter 8

65 Peterson, Jordan B. *12 Rules For Life: An Antidote to Chaos.* (Toronto: Random House Canada, 2018), 223.
66 Augustine. *Confessions.* (New York: Modern Library, 2017), 287.

Chapter 9

67 Delio, Ilia. *The Unbearable Wholeness of Being.* (Maryknoll: Orbis Books, 2013), 179-180.
68 *The Holy Bible: New International Version.* (Grand Rapids: Zondervan, 2011).
69 Buechner, Frederick. *The Magnificent Defeat.* (New York: Harper One, 1966), 32.
70 Ibid, 34.
71 *The Holy Bible: New International Version.* (Grand Rapids: Zondervan, 2011).

Afterword

72 Wilber, Ken. *Up From Eden.* (Wheaton: Quest Books, 1996), 16.
73 Delio, Ilia. *The Unbearable Wholeness of Being.* (Maryknoll: Orbis Books, 2013), 100-101.

A Final Exhortation

74 Climacus, John. *The Ladder of Divine Ascent.* (London: Harper & Bros., 1982), 208-209.